Rethinking Policing and Justice

It has become somewhat axiomatic to refer to the police as the 'gatekeepers' of the criminal justice system and thus as a mechanism for the provision of justice. And yet, when we conceptualize the police in this way, what is often taken for granted is the exact nature of that role and its larger social meaning. Indeed, we know that police deliver justice more efficiently to some and injustice to others. *Rethinking Policing and Justice* critically examines the role of policing (both state and non-state forms) in the provision of justice (and injustice). In essence, it presents work that highlights how different communities and groups have sought alternatives to policing, sometimes taking over the functions of policing. It also shows a variety of theoretical, methodology, and other approaches for the critical evaluation of law enforcement, highlighting different insights into alternative modes of policing, as we seek to understand and redraft the relationship between policing and justice.

This book was originally published as a special issue of *Contemporary Justice Review.*

Luis A. Fernandez is Associate Professor of Criminology and Criminal Justice at Northern Arizona University, USA. He is the author of several books, including *Policing Dissent: Social Control and the Anti-Globalization Movement* and *Shutting Down the Streets: Political Violence and Social Control in the Global Era.*

Laura Huey is Assistant Professor of Sociology at the University of Western Ontario, Canada. She is the author of several publications in the fields of policing, victimization and surveillance, including *Negotiating Demands: The Politics of Policing of Skid Row in Edinburgh, San Francisco and Vancouver.*

Rethinking Policing and Justice

Exploring Alternatives to Law Enforcement

Edited by

Luis A. Fernandez and Laura Huey

Routledge
Taylor & Francis Group
LONDON AND NEW YORK

First published 2012
by Routledge
2 Park Square, Milton Park, Abingdon, Oxon, OX14 4RN

Simultaneously published in the USA and Canada
by Routledge
711 Third Avenue, New York, NY 10017

Routledge is an imprint of the Taylor & Francis Group, an informa business

This book is a reproduction of *Contemporary Justice Review*, volume 14, issue 1. The Publisher requests to those authors who may be citing this book to state, also, the bibliographical details of the special issue on which the book was based.

British Library Cataloguing in Publication Data
A catalogue record for this book is available from the British Library

ISBN13: 978-0-415-69776-7 (hbk)

Typeset in Times New Roman
by Taylor & Francis Books

Disclaimer
The publisher would like to make readers aware that the chapters in this book are referred to as articles as they had been in the special issue. The publisher accepts responsibility for any inconsistencies that may have arisen in the course of preparing this volume for print.

Contents

Alternatives to policing

It has become somewhat axiomatic to refer to the police as the 'gatekeepers' of the criminal justice system and thus as a mechanism for the provision of justice. And yet, when we conceptualize the police thusly, what is often taken for granted is the exact nature of that role and its larger social meaning. Indeed, a number of scholars have argued that democratic policing systems can delivery some forms of justice within liberal regimes, but how the various symbolic and operational functions of the police serve the goal of justice remains a question of empirical research and debate. Certainly, we have also seen a wealth of scholarship that contests the view that public policing serves all equally, and thus is a questionable mechanism for accessing justice for each and every citizen. In other words, justice is delivered more efficiently to some folks and injustice to others. The latter perspective raises another whole series of questions as to possible alternatives to existing structures and processes that could make justice more widely accessible. For example, scholarship in this area has been near-exclusively focused on public policing, neglecting the plethora of private policing forms that operate beyond or below the state. Whether or to what extent such forms assist in providing access to justice (through the state or through private means) remains ill-understood.

Our goal in developing this special issue of *Contemporary Justice Review* was to explore issues related to the role of policing (both state and non-state forms) in the provision of justice. In essence, what we sought to create was a collection of papers that problematize this relationship, as well as developing new theoretical, methodological and other approaches for critically evaluating it. We also sought to create a space in which scholars could offer insights into alternative modes of 'policing' (broadly defined), which present us with new possibilities in understanding and redrafting the relationship of policing to justice.

In the pages that follow, readers will find articles that speak from a range of different perspectives and engage with a number of themes related to our core theme. The article that begins this collection is Marilyn Corsianos' 'Responding to officers' gendered experiences through community policing and improving police accountability to citizens', which highlights the issue of how the gendered, hierarchical nature of policing limits any real potential for reform in the areas of community service and public accountability. Corsianos argues for the meaningful implementation of community policing models as a means of not only flattening gendered, raced and other hierarchies within policing organizations to create better working environments for officers, but more importantly to engender ideological shifts necessary to improving police–community relations.

Various scholars have drawn our attention to the 'extended police family' (Johnston, 2003) and the ways in which policing functions are increasingly being taken up by actors within the private sector (Bayley & Shearing, 2001; Johnston & Shearing, 2003; Nogala, 2003). Only recently has that attention shifted to the role that community service providers are increasingly playing in policing 'below the state' (Eick, 2003; Huey, 2008). Volker Eick's 'Policing "below the state" in Germany: neocommunitarian soberness and punitive paternalism' contributes to this growing literature, sounding a dark warning as to the punitive side of altering relations between social workers and their clients, as the former are increasingly cast in the role of policing the latter.

Using observations drawn from ethnographic fieldwork to empirically ground her analysis, in 'The space between the steps: reckoning in an era of reconciliation', Michelle Stewart explores how efforts by members of Canada's Royal Canadian Mounted Police to create a community crime prevention forum became something very different for local residents. While constituted as a space to discuss the normal crimes of a community, it became a site in which participants instead discussed a shameful fact of Canada's past that lies at the root of many of the crimes within their community: the near-cultural genocide of the indigenous peoples and the lingering effects of the residential school system.

Drawing from his own recent research in this area, Michael Niman challenges our understanding of policing through an exploration of the work of the Rainbow Family, which utilizes pacificist forms of self-governance in their rehabilitative work with violent alcoholics. What the Rainbow family practises is, according to Niman, a form of 'police-less policing' with a demonstrably strong record of effectiveness within the community (p. 70). As Niman notes, this effectiveness can be ascribed to the fact that the community, as a whole, shares the values underpinning the 'policing philosophy'. Although this is a clear limitation of this model in relation to its potential for diffusion – not all cultures will ascribe to these same values – nevertheless the persistence of this 'utopian experiment' (p. 74) in the face of oppressive alternatives is cause for some hope.

Three research notes round out this special issue. The first examines another aspect of public policing – civilian oversight – that is assumed to be preferable to what is often the status quo, but is seldom rationalized by scholars. In 'Civilian oversight as a public good: democratic policing, civilian oversight, and the social', Danielle Hryniewicz draws on recent scholarship in security studies to articulate a sound theoretical basis for supporting civilian oversight of the public police, arguing that 'civilian oversight is a source of physical and ontological security' (p. 78).

Returning us to our concern with alternative policing modalities, Vikki Law explores the ways in which female-oriented grassroots groups and feminist activists have historically organized community alternatives to mobilizing police. Through an examination of some of the alternative practices developed, this abolitionist draws our attention to the need to engage in 'conversations on promoting safety and accountability without resorting to state-based policing and prisons' (p. 85).

We are fortunate to conclude this issue with a research note by Jeff Ferrell, in which he introduces the practice of 'corking'. 'Corking' represents, he suggests, an alternative mode of community policing, engaged in by Critical Mass activists seeking to raise awareness of environmental and other harms created by our obsessive love of the automobile.

We hope that readers will enjoy this special issue and find that the works contained here stimulate further thought and dialogue that will serve as an impetus to the development of new alternative approaches that will widen and strengthen the ability of citizens to access justice within their communities.

References

Bayley, D., & Shearing, C. (2001). *The new structure of policing: Description, conceptualization, agenda* (U.S. Department of Justice Research Report). Washington, DC: U.S. Department of Justice. Retrieved September 10, 2009, from http://www.ncjrs.gov/txtfiles1/nij/187083.txt

Eick, V. (2003). New strategies of policing the poor. *Policing & Society, 4*(13), 365–379.

Huey, L. (2008). 'When it comes to violence in my place, I am the police!' Exploring the policing functions of community service providers in Edinburgh's Cowgate and Grassmarket. *Policing & Society, 18*(3), 207–224.

Johnston, L. (2003). From 'pluralisation' to 'the police extended family': Discourses on the governance of community policing in Britain. *International Journal of the Sociology of Law, 31*(2), 185–204.

Johnston, L., & Shearing, C. (2003). *Governing security*. London: Routledge.

Nogala, D. (2003, February 19–22). *State, market, civil society: Mixing the economy of policing anew? Observations from Germany and continental Europe.* Paper presented at 'In Search of Security: An International Conference on Policing and Security', Montreal.

Laura Huey
Department of Sociology,
University of Western Ontario,
London, Ontario, Canada

Luis A. Fernandez
Department of Criminology and Criminal Justice,
Northern Arizona University,
Flagstaff, Arizona, USA

Responding to officers' gendered experiences through community policing and improving police accountability to citizens

Marilyn Corsianos

Department of Sociology, Anthropology and Criminology, Eastern Michigan University, 713K Pray Harrold, Ypsilanti, MI 48197, USA

This paper sets out to evaluate the potential for community policing (CP) to produce changes in gender equality in police agencies. To that end, the author evaluates if tenets of CP can create the necessary organizational and ideological changes required to move toward a post-gendered subjectivity in the work experiences of officers. If so, then CP tactics could be the start of changes of how traditional policing serves communities, opening a police–community partnership toward significant social change.

Introduction

By the early 1990s, large police departments in North America started to present community policing (CP) as the new central feature in their police operations largely in response to the police's ineffectiveness in reducing crime (Dietz, 1997; Rosenbaum, 1986; Skogan, 2004, 1996; Trojanowicz & Bucqueroux, 1990). Today, the majority of police agencies present themselves as operating on some level from a CP model (Greene, 2004; Roth, Roehl, & Johnson, 2004; Skogan, 1996, 1990). In fact, according to Skogan (2004), it is hard to find a police chief who does not claim to have adopted particular 'community-friendly programs.' But, despite the CP rhetoric and/or some CP initiatives, police organizations continue to reflect traditional dominant ideologies and the paramilitaristic power structure (Corsianos, 2009; Ericson & Haggerty, 1997; Manning, 1997; National Research Council, 2004; Skogan, 2004; Zhao, He, & Lovrich, 2003). As Greene (2004, p. 48) notes:

> The best that can be said to date is that many police departments .... have adopted a framework for response that includes elements of problem solving .... But ... it is clear that the police imagination remains captured by nineteenth-century ideas about crime and police response, most particularly as zero-tolerance policing has gained popularity among the police and politicians in recent years.

Clearly, the research on CP since the early 1990s has been significant, but, what is also clear is that police agencies have not been transformed into collectivist, non-patriarchal, and non-hierarchical CP organizations that promote teamwork among all ranks, the well-being of officers by treating them equally regardless of 'identity categories,' such as gender (as well as others such as sexual orientation, race, ethnicity, etc.) and ensure police accountability and teamwork with communities to address crimes and other community concerns (Goetz & Mitchell, 2003; Greene, 2004; MacDonald, 2002; Martin & Jurik, 2007; Roth et al., 2004; Skogan, 2004; Thacher, 2001; Wyrick, 2000; Zhao et al., 2003; and others).

Overall, police officers continue to work in a traditional, hierarchical, paramilitaristic police structure that promotes aggressive crime control, reactive policing, hypermasculinity, obedience to the chain of command, and fixed rigid operating systems. Thus, policing methods have largely remained the same as in previous decades (Corsianos, 2009, 2001; Ericson, 1994; Ericson & Haggerty, 1997; Greene, 2004; Manning, 1997; National Research Council, 2004; Neugebauer, 1999; Roth et al., 2004; Skogan, 2004; Zhao et al., 2003), and the current organizational structure and culture continue to produce gendered differences in the experiences of officers (Corsianos, 2009; Harrington & Lonsway, 2004; Martin & Jurik, 2007; Morash & Harr, 1995).

Although, the CP model was not introduced with the intention of addressing and changing the gendered experiences of officers, this paper will set out to critically evaluate how specific tenets of CP, if integrated throughout the entire organization, can create the necessary organizational and ideological changes required to move toward a post-gendered subjectivity in the work experiences of officers, which in turn can then begin to change the ways police serve communities. In other words, the question that is raised is whether CP can create the necessary changes needed to identify and remove discriminatory practices and attitudes and promote gender equity for all officers and, in turn, begin to redefine police organizations in ways that promote police–community partnerships, transparency, and accountability on the part of the police. The paper will begin by examining how the current organizational structure and culture produce gendered differences in the experiences of American and Canadian officers and will then assess the potential for CP to redefine policing internally by positively responding to the uneven power relations between officers and ultimately the uneven power relations between communities and law enforcement agencies.

How do police organizations produce gendered differences in the experiences of officers?

In the USA today, women constitute approximately 13% of all police officers (National Center for Women and Policing, 2003; United States Department of Labor, 2007) and in Canada, 17% (Statistics Canada, 2005). These percentages are not surprising given the gendered experiences within policing. Even though many police departments claim to promote equity and foster a supportive work environment for all its employees, few have taken the necessary steps to examine how their current organizational structure and ideologies promote gendered experiences among officers. For instance, women officers have been subjected to discriminatory policies and practices; various sexist, heterosexist, and/or racist comments; sexual harassment and assault; intimidation; retaliation; derogatory comments made regarding their competency/ability to be effective law enforcers; criticism regarding their physical strength, height, and/or the ability to protect themselves and other officers in physical confrontations with members of the public; chivalrous attitudes; pressure to prove themselves and conform to the status quo; and discrimination in hiring, position assignments and promotions (Belknap, 1991; Corsianos, 2004, 2009; Fielding, 1994; Feinman, 1986; Gerber, 2001; Harrington & Lonsway, 2004; Heidensohn & Brown, 2000; Homant &

Kennedy, 1985; Kennedy & Homant, 1983; Martin, 1980, 1994, 1999; Martin & Jurik, 2007; Miller, 1999; Morash & Greene, 1986; Nichols, 1995; Price, 1974; Robinson, 1993; Van Wormer & Bartollas, 2000). Additionally, female officers who are perceived as 'deviant' or 'rocking the boat' are closely policed by management whereas others who frequently appropriate the patriarchal tools used to stroke the egos of those in the upper ranks are often rewarded (Corsianos, 2004).

The gender roles displayed within police organizations are informed by what Fielding (1994), Messerschmidt (1993, 2003), and others describe as 'hegemonic masculinity.' Masculine characteristics are assumed to be central to the roles of the police officer and are accepted as 'common sense.' Female officers are perceived as lacking 'masculine' traits that are believed to be crucial for officers, particularly aggressiveness, bravery, rationality, objectivity, and brutality (Charles, 1981; Miller, 1999). These often lead to claims that women are inherently not able to perform the duties identified under the crime-fighting police model and that they are better suited to police roles that deal with social service-type functions (Bell, 1982; Drummond, 1976; Heidensohn, 1992; Heidensohn & Brown, 2000). This is despite the fact that most police work involves 'social work' types of activities (Martin, 1999; Walker & Katz, 2005). But, despite this, police agencies place a higher value on officers' arrest rates and types of arrests.

Police operations often involve activities that are 'feminine' (Belknap, 2007; Martin, 1999; Martin & Jurik, 2007), but, they largely remain unrecognized by police organizations. Some academics have found that female police officers have a less aggressive style than male officers and are better at de-escalating potentially violent situations (Belknap, 1991; Belknap & Shelley, 1993; Bell, 1982; Grennan, 1987). Also, female officers are more likely to have traits associated with 'good policing,' such as expressing empathy for victims of violence (Feinman, 1986; Homant & Kennedy, 1985; Kennedy & Homant, 1983; Price, 1974). But, this information is not utilized by police organizations to improve training or to reassess their overwhelming focus on arrests.

Furthermore, specialized police units continue to be gendered. A disproportionate number of women are employed in CP, domestic violence, sexual assault, and youth bureaus/units; alternatively, a disproportionate number of male officers are often found in homicide units, vice, specialized tactical units, and fraud (Boni, 1998; Heidensohn & Brown, 2000; Martin & Jurik, 2007; Ness & Gordon, 1995; Schulz, 2004). Not surprisingly, the units that become 'feminized' are often not seen as 'real police work' (Miller, 1999). The recent feminization of particular policing areas such as CP, coupled with the fact that they typically do not produce high-speed chases or 'big arrests,' perpetuates the belief that the work of officers in these units is somehow less important, serving to further ostracize female officers (Corsianos, 2009). Also, other studies have found that male officers perceive the more 'feminized' areas/units, such as CP, as being synonymous with 'social work' since they conflict with the image of the police as crime fighters; in turn, many reject opportunities to work in a CP capacity (Miller & Hodge, 2004).

Police organizations in North America have also overall not been successful in creating a more family-friendly work environment which disproportionately affects female officers. For instance, most police officers work rotating shifts and do not have the option to choose any one fixed schedule which presents several challenges to police officers who are mothers and, more specifically, single mothers. Given that women continue to take on more child care issues, this negatively impacts a disproportionate number of women. For these reasons, Corsianos (2009) found that American and Canadian female officers supported a system that would allow officers with young children to work permanent shifts until their children were old enough to be home without adult supervision; and in cases where both parents were police officers, only one parent could be given this option. Moreover, they also supported on-site childcare centers during the day shift as well as temporary part-time status for officers with family needs or other personal circumstances.

Additionally, many American police organizations have not introduced clearly defined pregnancy/maternity policies relating to one or more of the following: police maternity uniforms, suitable maternity police equipment (e.g., bulletproof vests, gun belts), 'light duty,' or non-patrol assignments, and postnatal nursing policies (for nursing officers who have returned to work). At the same time, some departments require officers to requalify on the shooting range during their pregnancies without the necessary safety precautions. Many officers have refused to qualify on the range due to their concerns relating to the possible harm to the fetus resulting from the consequent high noise level and lead pollution (Harrington & Lonsway, 2004; Martin & Jurik, 2007).

Moreover, gendered differences are experienced in the areas of hiring, promotions and performance evaluations. For instance, in many American police departments, oral interview boards consist mainly of current male officers who are not screened for personal biases and therefore bring their own prejudices into the interview to determine whether applicants possess the qualities of a 'good police officer' needed for promotion or to gain access to specialized units. Thus, it is not uncommon for women to receive lower scores from these boards because their work experiences, which may include backgrounds in social services, childcare, and education, are not as valued as those of individuals (mostly males) who have backgrounds in the military or security services and because these boards do not equally value all aspects of policing experience including service in all units/areas, completion of internal specialized courses, completion of university/college courses, community service, awards received, letters of recommendation, etc. (Corsianos, 2004; Harrington & Lonsway, 2004; Martin, 1990). In some Canadian police departments, collective agreements specify how temporary position assignments and deployment to special projects should be done in an attempt to solve the challenges women have faced in gaining access. But, as Josiah (1997, p. 84) notes: 'There may be unintentional barriers to women's increased participation; these should be examined closely by police services boards, labor and management, with adequate representation of women on the working group.' For instance, Corsianos (2009) found that officers were typically given the opportunity to serve in detective units in temporary training positions. But, decisions regarding the permanent detective positions were made secretly before the official job post was advertised throughout the organization and were based largely on perceptions of who was considered a 'team player.'

Moreover, women with childcare responsibilities are at a disadvantage since they cannot regularly socialize with other officers after work. It is believed that this form of networking also plays a key role in who is ultimately promoted. On the surface, the promotional process appears to be objective. However, in actuality, decisions relating to who is promoted are based on discriminatory practices and are often made before the formal interview process begins (Harrington & Lonsway, 2004; Martin & Jurik, 2007).

With regard to performance evaluation criteria, they may appear on the surface to be gender-neutral but may end up being based on men's performance standards.

Martin (1990), for example, found that performance evaluation criteria used in assessing 'quantity of work' in the Chicago Police Department included only number of arrests, court attendance, traffic enforcement, and award history. Also, Harrington and Lonsway (2004) found that women's successes in crime prevention, proactive policing, and working with specific communities, as well as victims of crime, are not valued as much as are the types of activities that produce arrests and thus women working in these capacities are at a disadvantage when evaluated.

Also, most police organizations continue to place value on a rather narrow definition of 'physical strength' which continues to support the image of the police as 'crime fighters' and the accompanying aggressive, paramilitaristic crime control tactics. Many American agencies continue to have standards that place a strong emphasis on upper body strength (Harrington & Lonsway, 2004; National Center for Women and Policing, 2005). But, these tests do not measure police competency in day-to-day police activities, and they disproportionately discriminate against women. Ironically, many departments have written policies that prohibit some of these physical activities, such as jumping over solid walls or indicate that they are inadvisable. Yet, some organizations continue to perceive these tests as appropriate and/or effective measures of police officer performance (Harrington & Lonsway, 2004). Most police agencies, in both the USA and Canada, claim that certain physical testing during the application process is required in order to hire individuals capable of doing the job of a police officer. But, once hired, officers in both of these countries are no longer subject to routine physical testing and thus there is no way of knowing whether they can still meet these 'standards.' Yet, their ability to serve as officers is no longer questioned. Also, in a 2001 US study, 89% of 62 large police agencies used some form of physical agility testing as a condition for hiring, but there was little standardization with regard to the actual physical tests and the measurements used to receive a pass. Given the gender bias in some of these physical tests, it is not surprising to see that departments that did not indicate the use of any physical tests as a condition for employment had 45% more women serving as sworn police officers (National Center for Women and Policing, 2003). Clearly, police organizations produce and reproduce gendered experiences on the part of officers, but, given police departments' continued promotion of CP as central to their policing practices (Greene, 2004; MacDonald, 2002; Morash & Robinson, 2002; Roth et al., 2004; Skogan, 2004; Wyrick, 2000; Zdanowicz, 2001), the questions that must be asked are how can the police be expected to be accountable to communities and be willing to equitably serve citizens when they do not promote equitable practices and ideologies within the organization? Also, how can the police be expected to equitably and collectively work with communities when so-called 'feminine' traits, which are central to building bridges between the police and the public, are not valued? The next section will critically evaluate how the CP model can promote gender equity which can then ultimately improve police service to communities.

Promoting gender equality through CP and improving accountability to communities

CP is intended to shift the emphasis away from the traditional mechanistic model of policing that focuses on law enforcement and aggressive crime control, limited public interaction, motorized random patrol, reactive policing, and a centralized dispatching of radio calls that are supported by a hierarchical, paramilitaristic organizational structure. CP has been described as policing organized around perspectives that not only emphasize crime control and order-maintenance, but also emphasize more diverse approaches such as crime prevention, proactive policing, community problem-solving, improvement of police–community relations by reducing the social distance between the police and the public through increased police accountability and improved service to the public, empowerment of front-line officers, and a flatter organizational power structure that promotes team work and a collectivist spirit among all officers.

It is also intended to redefine police organizations and move away from the image of the police as 'aggressive crime fighters,' 'macho' and having a sense of being 'above the law' and/or sense of entitlement over citizens. It can be argued that CP calls for more 'feminine' characteristics on the part of officers including, but not limited, being able to de-escalate potentially violent situations, being effective communicators, expressing empathy for victims of crime, being good listeners when dealing with citizens' complaints and/or concerns, and working collectively with citizens to identify problems in particular neighborhoods as well as solutions.

But, attempts must be made by police departments to integrate the CP model throughout their entire organization rather than creating specialized CP units. For example in Miller's (1999) study of a Midwestern police department, officers were either patrol officers or neighborhood policing officers (NPOs). Miller reported that this particular organization had CP for a decade, and 10 years after its inception the program had expanded from the original six to twelve neighborhoods, but, there was still tension between patrol and neighborhood officers. She described the tension to be the result of at least two reasons: one being confusion and misunderstanding of the work of NPOs, and the second was the tendency to see these positions as 'stepping stones' to getting promoted. Also, many of the NPOs felt the pressure to gain more respect from the patrol officers and one of the strategies used was to increase their law enforcement visibility and to be seen less as social workers. This divided police officers as one group worked to gain acceptance and legitimacy by the other who was perceived as doing more normative police work. This, unfortunately, does not help to change the current dominant image of the police as 'crime fighters' to one centered on representing and serving communities.

Under the CP model, there must be constant interaction and cooperation between all police officers and the public, and not just particular specialized CP units. This, in turn, produces information-sharing which not only increases the likelihood of arrest, but also calls on the police to work with citizens to address violations of the social order – the idea being that if visible signs of disorder are reduced, so, too, are crimes and the fear of crime (Bayley, 1988, 1994; Goldstein, 1990, 1977; Spelman & Eck, 1987; Trojanowicz, 1983; Trojanowicz & Bucqueroux, 1990; Wilson & Kelling, 1982). Additionally, it advocates more indirect approaches to social control and limits the number of arrests made. Also, it calls for the recognition that not all communities may be the same (even within the patrol parameters of a particular precinct) and that all front-line police officers must address the different 'public safety' needs identified by different groups (Thacher, 2001).

Thus, in moving away from the image of the police as paramilitaristic and promoting open communication between the police and citizens, the CP model emphasizes post-secondary education for officers rather than the traditional military and security experiences. For instance, the Vancouver police department has been a strong supporter of the CP model for the last two decades plus. In the 1990s, it began to challenge the image of their department as being synonymous with crime control and brawn. Rather than giving points to applicants for having military and security experience, they identified four preferred qualifications for the job of police officer. Two of the four included a university degree or a college diploma and a second language or culture (Eng, 1997). It can be argued then that under the CP model, there should be more emphasis on hiring officers with diverse skills who are critical thinkers and have a university/college education that will benefit them as officers (e.g., have taken courses on race and ethnicity, sex and gender, class inequalities, languages, social stratification, sexuality, social problems, conflict resolution, etc.) as well as eliminating the use of physical testing used for hiring that emphasizes upper body strength and does not reflect the day-to-day job of community-friendly officers.

The traditional, hierarchical, mechanistic police model emphasizes crime control through law enforcement and promotes hypermasculinity (Martin & Jurik, 2007). However, under the CP model, crime control is presented as the product of the combined efforts of both the police and the public, and more 'feminine' traits become central in accomplishing the goals of the organization. The latter is intended to encourage information exchange and support from the public and quick police response to the public's concerns (Eck, 1990; Eck & Spelman, 1987; Jolin & Moose, 1997; Morash & Robinson, 2002; Zdanowicz, 2001).

Moreover, CP advocates a flatter power structure within the police organization, that is, a downward shift of the command structure to empower the front-line officers by encouraging them to engage in critical thinking and problem-solving. The organizational structure is described as being more fluidic where every member of the organization is seen as a team player and possesses some knowledge of the organization. Every individual has *some knowledge* rather than the hierarchical model where the people at the top of the pyramid are described as having knowledge of the entire organization. Emphasis is placed on shared responsibility where every police officer is expected to contribute to organizational problems (Bayley, 1988; Chalom, 1993; Cordner, 1994; Goetz & Mitchell, 2003; Goldstein, 1990; Greene, 2004; Guarino-Ghezzi, 1994; Macdonald, 2002; Manning, 1997; Skogan, 1990, 1996; Stenson, 1993; Trojanowicz & Bucqueroux, 1990). The flatter power structure can create equitable practices. It would ensure that all front-line officers are given a voice and valued more equally (which would affect a disproportionate number of women seeing that the majority currently occupy the lower ranks) (National Center for Women and Policing, 2001; Statistics Canada, 2005) and increase management's accountability to them. The success of CP depends largely on the efficacy of the font-line officer. Therefore, the CP platform could be used by female officers to voice concerns within the department and bring some of their issues and experiences to the forefront. Specific structural organizational changes could be introduced to address these concerns and provide officers with choices. These would give way to the creation of a more supportive work environment and improve morale. In turn, more women would be encouraged to become police officers and stay on until retirement since it appears that police departments have more trouble retaining female officers (Doerner, 1996; IACP, 1998; Los Angeles Police Commission, 2000; Schultz, 2004).

The focus under CP is on the 'ends,' that is, getting the job done because every member is seen as a competent professional who can be trusted to make good decisions in specific situations. This model allows for more discretionary powers to individual officers by limiting the degree of restrictions placed on police discretion. But, at the same time, this requires trust on the part of the officers to ensure that they do not abuse their powers and will be committed to serving citizens equitably and respectfully. Moreover, interaction among officers is more inclusive and horizontal. Rather than 'obeying' the 'chain of command' and taking orders from 'superiors' (reflective of the paramilitaristic, hierarchical police structure), the CP approach encourages a style of communication that is more collectivist-oriented where people receive 'advice' rather than 'orders,' and thus officers are expected to work together to achieve particular goals. These collectivist approaches are believed to promote team work, open communication, transparency, accountability, and even out the power relations between officers (Bayley, 1988; Corsianos, 2009; Goldstein, 1990; Manning, 1997; Miller, 1999; Morash & Robinson, 2002; Spelman & Eck, 1987; Thacher, 2001; Trojanowicz & Bucqueroux, 1990; Wyrick, 2000; Zdanowicz, 2001). Once again, this can promote gender equity by giving a voice to all officers more equally.

Under the CP model, officers are expected to have good interpersonal skills and be trained in problem identification, analysis, and solutions (Jurik & Martin, 2001). This can promote gender equity by promoting traits that are disproportionately associated with female officers (e.g., they are less likely to use excessive force, less likely to be involved in other forms of police corruption, are better able to de-escalate potentially violent situations, communicate effectively, etc.). The front-line officer is expected to play a central role in the success of CP given that front-line officers are the ones who are in constant contact with communities. Unlike members of upper management, the front-line/patrol officers work 'on the streets' and can gain a better understanding of the needs and concerns of the public. In turn, they can bring this information to management which can lead to substantive action plans. This is not typical under the traditional police structure that requires front-line officers to take any information to their immediate 'superiors' and not 'break rank' by going to persons above them. For these reasons, good interpersonal skills and the ability to work with citizens to identify and solve problems are crucial.

Additionally, under the CP model, police departments will move away from the current police organizational structure and operational systems which ultimately serve to maintain male privilege. The current structure and systems undermine female officers because they have been set up in ways that do not recognize and respond to the socially constructed realities of categories of people. As reported in Corsianos's study (2009), female officers who were mothers experienced difficulties in balancing shift work with child-rearing responsibilities. Also, many officers identified problems with gender-specific assignments, the emphasis on physical strength in hiring, and the negative impact on women working in policing units that typically did not generate arrests. Alternatively, the CP model has the potential of making the connection between 'identity categories' and differences in people's experiences and thus is able to promote equitable practices and real change in the experiences of officers. But, all police departments would be required to commit to an equity analysis of all police policies and practices to ensure that no category of officers (e.g., women and other groups) was disproportionately discriminated against. The implementation of the CP model throughout the entire organization would begin to change the current dominant image of the police.

The promotion of CP can lead to ideological shifts in both the officers' and the public's perceptions of what a police officer *should look like* and how a police officer *should behave.* At the same time, police departments must continue to examine the conditional 'truths' that people rely on to actively build their social world (Henry &

Milovanovic, 1999), and police organizations must respond by implementing policies and practices that benefit all diverse groups. For example, as mentioned earlier, performance evaluations that are included in officers' evaluations for promotion lack procedures that recognize and reward officers' work outside of law enforcement/crime control roles. This produces gendered results, since accomplishments that are highly valued by many women officers such as CP, working with victims of crime, etc. are virtually unrecognized by the current police system and culture. This is very significant since law enforcement comprises only a small part of everyday police work (Martin, 1999; Walker & Katz, 2005). Also, as discussed earlier, CP initiatives are not recognized and valued as are traditional policing roles that produce a high number of arrests. Male officers continue to perceive CP as 'women's work' that contradicts the image of the police as law enforcers and crime fighters, and they continue to turn down opportunities to work in these units (Miller & Hodge, 2004). But, interestingly, for the male officers who do work in CP, they are often given more recognition in relation to their female counterparts. For instance, Miller (1999) found that in comparison to male officers, women received less credit for their accomplishments in CP. The expectation is often that women should be better in CP roles given their gender roles and thus are not rewarded equally (Miller, 1999).

Moreover, police organizations currently promote authoritarianism, aggressiveness, paramilitarism, secrecy, respect for the chain of command, hypermasculinity, and the ideology of the 'brotherhood of policing' (Birzer & Tannehill, 2001; Crank, 1998; Dixon, 1992; Fyfe, 1991; Goldsmith, 1990; Manning, 1997; Scripture, 1997; Storch & Panzarella, 1996). But, a genuine commitment to CP throughout the entire organization could replace these with a collective community-oriented ideology that promotes collectivism, equitable policies that incorporate an equity analysis to ensure that police policies do not disproportionately discriminate against categories of people (e.g., in hiring, promotions, performance evaluations, position assignments, police equipment, training, work schedules, parental leave, etc.) and could promote police–community partnerships and police accountability. This would encourage more women to apply and ultimately lead to more female representation in all aspects of policing. There would be no place for chivalrous attitudes, sexist stereotypes, and other discriminatory practices that are overwhelmingly reported in the research (Belknap & Shelley, 1993; Corsianos, 2009; Garcia, 2003; Gerber, 2001; Jackson, 1997; Martin, 1999; Martin & Jurik, 2007; McLean, 1997; Morash & Greene, 1986; Orban, 1998; Prokos & Padavic, 2002).

A commitment to this ideology will promote gender equity and, overtime, create the cultural space for a post-gendered subjectivity. But, identifying and removing the various instances of discriminatory police rhetoric, images, and police practices are key. Police officers are individuals who make observations day in and day out. They are continuously observing and interpreting the occupational systems, structures, and internal power dynamics. Thus, the current organizational power structure that produces and promotes difference in outcome of welfare among its officers undermines the potential for a post-gendered subjectivity which in turn undermines the potential to effectively respond to the uneven power relations between the police and communities.

Also, as mentioned earlier, the CP model promotes continuous educational courses for officers and improved diverse courses at police academies/colleges as well as post-secondary education as a requirement for officers. This is an important tenet of the CP model. Thus, recognizing that education is central to consciousness-raising and promoting social change (Bannerji, Carty, Dehli, Heald, & McKenna, 1991; Das Gupta, 1994; Scheurich & Young, 2002), and restructuring courses taught at police colleges/academies would be an important step. Different experiences and perspectives should be integrated into the core curricula. Reading material, class lectures, and classroom structure should represent all students, and diverse voices must be integrated into police training. 'Knowledge' of policing must be the product of combined diverse perspectives, rather than the voice of a few white males as is currently the case. In other words, the perspectives and experiences of one particular group should not be privileged over others. Also, 'special topics' training that includes gender and LGBT relations, human sensitivity training, race and ethnic relations, etc. must not be treated as 'add-ons' to general training or as being less serious or insignificant. Topics treated as 'add-ons' serve to maintain the power and influence of the current policing 'knowledge.' The above-mentioned subject areas must become integrated into all aspects of police training, rather than being allotted only a few hours as classroom presentations.

Also, some studies show that police officers who hold a college degree are less likely to participate in acts of police corruption and are more likely to be fair and honest (Hoover, 1995; Lynch, 1976). They are also less likely to receive citizen complaints and are more likely to have fewer disciplinary problems (Carter, Sapp, & Stephens, 1988). Hiring more people with college/university degrees in the humanities and social sciences may mean hiring officers who are more tolerant of diversity and more aware of the socially constructed differences in the experiences of categories of people. Exposure to these types of 'knowledge' prior to becoming police officers may increase the likelihood of achieving long-term CP goals, internally and externally, rather than working with recruits who have had no prior exposure and/or are hostile toward them. It is believed that more educated officers are more likely to interact positively with the people they work with and the communities they serve.

Furthermore, by recognizing every police role as an integral part to the overall police system, police organizations could begin to move away from the gendered division of labor we often see within police departments today. The flat power structure promoted under the CP model would ensure that everyone had an equal chance of serving in all areas within policing and would recognize officers' good work in all aspects of policing through awards, appreciation ceremonies, and internal newsletter announcements. This would include the contributions of officers in decreasing crimes as a result of the successful implementation of CP initiatives or victim–offender mediation. Also, managers would be required to promote the CP model in all aspects of policing. This would send the message that arrest rates are not the only way to measure police performance and success. These could produce the needed ideological shift within policing that currently discriminates against certain types of police activities. Thus, more male officers would be encouraged to work in areas that have become associated with female officers and vice versa. This would help free all police officers from the current gendered societal and departmental expectations as every interested police officer would have an equal chance of serving in all areas of policing, and the current dominant police practices would start to change.

By integrating the CP model throughout the entire organization, the experienced gender inequalities of police officers can be identified and removed. But, the dominant internal practices must be re-evaluated and pursued simultaneously in association with an interrogation of the current organizational structure. Police organizations produce and promote differences in outcome of welfare among its officers and undermine the potential for a post-gendered subjectivity. However, by evaluating and changing the ideological and central structural arrangements in police organizations, social categories, such as gender will no longer serve as barriers to equal access and employment experiences. But, changes have to be made at both the micro and macro structural levels. The continuous promotion of equitable politics is necessary in order to encourage equitable praxis. These changes will help resocialize officers and lead to the necessary ideological shifts required to accomplish police–community partnerships, equitable police service, and accountability to communities.

References

Bannerji, H., Carty, L., Dehli, K., Heald, S., & McKenna, S. (1991). *Unsettling relations: The university as a site of feminist struggle.* Toronto: Women's Press.

Bayley, D.H. (1988). Community policing: A report from the devil's advocate. In J.R. Greene & S.D. Mastrofski (Eds.), *Community policing: Rhetoric or reality* (pp. 225–238). New York: Praeger.

Bayley, D.H. (1994). *Police for the future.* New York: Oxford University Press.

Belknap, J. (1991). Women in conflict: An analysis of women correctional officers. *Women and Criminal Justice, 2*, 89–115.

Belknap, J. (2007). *The invisible woman: Gender, crime and justice* (3rd ed.). Belmont, CA: Thomson Wadsworth.

Belknap, J., & Shelley, J.K. (1993). The new lone ranger: Policewomen on patrol. *American Journal of Police, 12*, 47–75.

Bell, D.J. (1982). Policewomen: myths and realities. *Journal of Police Science and Administration, 10*(1), 112–120.

Birzer, M., & Tannehill, R. (2001). A more effective training approach for contemporary policing. *Police Quarterly, 4*(2), 233–252.

Boni, N. (1998). *Deployment of women in policing.* Payneham: National Police Research Unit.

Carter, D., Sapp, A., & Stephens, D. (1988). *The state of police education: Policy direction for the 21st century.* Washington, DC: Police Executive Research Forum.

Chalom, M. (1993). Community policing: Toward a new paradigm of prevention? *International Review of Community Development, 30*(70), 155–161.

Charles, M.T. (1981). The performance and socialization of female recruits in the Michigan State police training academy. *Journal of Police Science and Administration, 9*, 209–223.

Cordner, G. (1994). Foot patrol without community policing: Law and order in public housing. In D. Rosenbaum (Ed.), *The challenge of community policing: Testing the promises* (pp. 182–191). Thousand Oaks, CA: Sage.

Corsianos, M. (2001). Conceptualizing 'justice' in detectives' decision making. *International Journal of the Sociology of Law, 29*(2), 113–126.

Corsianos, M. (2004). 'Women' detectives and perceptions of 'oppressive' experiences: Exploring experiential essentialism and phenomenology. *Critical Criminology, 12*(1), 67–85.

Corsianos, M. (2009). *Policing and gendered justice: Examining the possibilities.* Toronto: University of Toronto Press.

Crank, J. (1998). *Understanding police culture.* Cincinnati, OH: Anderson.

Das Gupta, T. (1994). Towards an anti-racist, feminist teaching method. *Feminism and Education: A Canadian Perspective, 2*, 17–42.

Dietz, A. (1997). Evaluating community policing: Quality police service and fear of crime. *Policing: An International Journal of Police Strategies and Management, 20*(1), 83–100.

Dixon, D. (1992). Legal regulation and policing practice. *Social and Legal Studies, 1*(4), 515–541.

Doerner, W.G. (1996). Officer retention patterns: An affirmative action concern for police agencies. *American Journal of Police, 14*, 205.

Drummond, D.S. (1976). *Police culture.* Thousand Oaks, CA: Sage.

Eck, J.E. (1990). A realistic approach to controlling drug harms. *Public Management,* 7–12.

Eck, J.E., & Spelman, W. (1987). Who ya gonna call: The police as problem-busters. *Crime & Delinquency, 33*(1), 31–52.

Eng, S. (1997, May). *Policies for women in the justice field – Need or necessity.* A presentation made at the women in policing in Canada: The year 2000 and beyond – Its challenges workshop, Canadian Police College, Ottawa, ON.
Ericson, R. (1994). The division of expert knowledge in policing and security. *British Journal of Sociology, 45*(2), 149–175.
Ericson, R., & Haggerty, K. (1997). *Policing the risk society.* Toronto: University of Toronto Press.
Feinman, C. (1986). *Women in the criminal justice system.* New York: Praeger.
Fielding, N. (1994). Cop canteen culture. In T. Newburn & E.A. Stanko (Eds.), *Just boys doing business? Men, masculinities and crime* (pp. 46–62). London: Routledge.
Fyfe, N.R. (1991). The police, space and society: The geography of policing. *Progress in Human Geography, 15*(3), 249–267.
Garcia, V. (2003). 'Difference' in the policing department: Women, policing, and 'doing gender.' *Journal of Contemporary Criminal Justice, 19*, 330–344.
Gerber, G.L. (2001). *Women and men police officers: Status, gender and personality.* New York: Praeger.
Goetz, B., & Mitchell, R. (2003). Community-building and reintegrative approaches to community policing: The case of drug control. *Social Justice, 30*(1), 222–247.
Goldsmith, A. (1990). Taking police culture seriously: Police discretion and the limits of law. *Policing and Society, 1*(2), 91–114.
Goldstein, H. (1977). *Policing a free society.* Cambridge, MA: Ballinger.
Goldstein, H. (1990). *Problem-oriented policing.* New York: McGraw-Hill.
Greene, J.R. (2004). Community policing and police organization. In W.G. Skogan (Ed.), *Community policing (can it work?)* (pp. 30–54). Belmont, CA: Thomson Wadsworth.
Grennan, S.A. (1987). Findings on the role of officer gender in violent encounters with citizens. *Journal of Police Science and Administration, 15*, 78–85.
Guarino-Ghezzi, S. (1994). Reintegrative police surveillance of juvenile offenders: Forging an urban model. *Crime and Delinquency, 40*, 131–153.
Harrington, P., & Lonsway, K.A. (2004). Current barriers and future promise for women in policing. In B.R. Price and N.J. Sokoloff (Eds.), *The criminal justice system and women: Offenders, prisoners, victims, & workers* (3rd ed.). New York: McGraw Hill.
Heidensohn, F.M. (1992). *Women in control? The role of women in law enforcement.* New York: Oxford University Press.
Heidensohn, F., & Brown, J. (2000). *Gender and policing: Comparative perspectives.* New York: St. Martin's Press.
Henry, S., & Milovanovic, D. (1999). *Constitutive criminology at work.* Albany, NY: State University of New York Press.
Homant, R., & Kennedy, D. (1985). Police perceptions of spouse abuse: A comparison of male and female officers. *Journal of Criminal Justice, 13*(1), 29–47.
Hoover, L. (1995). Education. In W.G. Bailey (Ed.), *The encyclopedia of police science* (pp. 245–248, 2nd ed.). New York: Garland.
International Association of Chiefs of Police (IACP). (1998). *The future of women in policing: Mandates for action.* Retrieved from www.theiacp.org/Portals/0/pdfs/Publications/ACF830.pdf
Jackson, L.D. (1997, May). *Crossing the thin blue line: A study of female police officers in Atlantic Canada.* A presentation made at the women in policing in Canada: The Year 2000 and beyond – Its challenges workshop, Canadian Police College, Ottawa, ON.
Jolin, A., & Moose, C.A. (1997). Evaluating a domestic violence program in a community policing environment: Research implementation issues. *Crime and Delinquency, 43*, 279–297.
Josiah, H. (1997, May). *Innovative policy development approaches.* A presentation made at the women in policing in Canada: The year 2000 and beyond – Its challenges workshop, Canadian Police College, Ottawa, ON.
Jurik, N.C., & Martin, S.E. (2001). Femininities, masculinities and organizational conflict: Women in criminal justice occupations. In C.M. Renzetti & L. Goodstein (Eds.), *Women, crime and criminal justice.* Los Angeles, CA: Roxbury.
Kennedy, D., & Homant, R. (1983). Attitudes of abused women toward male and female police officers. *Criminal Justice and Behavior, 10*, 391–405.

Los Angeles Police Commission. (2000). *Police academy and probationary officer attrition.* Retrieved from www.lapdonline.org/police_commission
Lynch, G. (1976). Contributions of higher education to ethical behavior in law enforcement. *Journal of Criminal Justice, 4*(4), 285–290.
MacDonald, J.M. (2002). The effectiveness of community policing in reducing urban violence. *Crime & Delinquency, 48*(4), 592–618.
Manning, P.K. (1997). *Police work: The social organization of policing* (2nd ed.). Prospect Heights, IL: Waveland Press.
Martin, S.E. (1980). *Breaking and entering: Policewomen on patrol.* Berkeley, CA: University of California Press.
Martin, S.E. (1990). *On the move: The status of women in policing.* Washington, DC: Police Foundation.
Martin, S.E. (1994). Outsider within the station house: The impact of race and gender on Black women police. *Social Problems, 41*(3), 383–400.
Martin, S.E. (1999). Police force or police service? Gender and emotional labor. *Annals of the American Academy of Political & Social Science, 561,* 111–126.
Martin, S.E., & Jurik, N.C. (2007). *Doing justice, doing gender: Women in legal and criminal justice occupations* (2nd ed.). Thousand Oaks, CA: Sage.
McLean, J. (1997, May). *The effects of the police culture on social identity.* A presentation made at the women in policing in Canada: The year 2000 and beyond – Its challenges workshop, Canadian Police College, Ottawa, ON.
Messerschmidt, J. (1993). *Masculinities and crime: Critique and reconceptualization of theory.* Landham, MD: Rowman & Littlefield.
Messerschmidt, J. (2003). Diversity in blue: Lesbian and gay police officers in a masculine occupation. *Men and Masculinities, 5*(4), 355–385.
Miller, S.L. (1999). *Gender and community policing: Walking the talk.* Boston, MA: Northeastern University Press.
Miller, S.L., & Hodge, J. (2004). Rethinking gender and community policing: Cultural obstacles and policy issues. *Law Enforcement Executive Forum. 44*, 39–49.
Morash, M., & Greene, J.R. (1986). Evaluating women on patrol: A critique of contemporary wisdom. *Evaluation Review, 10*(2), 230–255.
Morash, M., & Harr, R.N. (1995). Gender, workplace problems and stress in policing. *Justice Quarterly, 12*(1), 113–140.
Morash, M., & Robinson, A.L. (2002). Correctional administrators' perspectives on gender arrangements and family-related programming for women offenders. *Marriage and the Family Review, 32*(3–4), 83–109.
National Center for Women and Policing. (2001). *Equality denied: The status of women in policing: 2001.* Feminist Majority Foundation. Retrieved from http://www.womeninpolicing.org/PDF/2002_Status_Report.pdf
National Center for Women and Policing. (2003). *Under scrutiny: The effect of consent decrees on the representation of women in sworn law enforcement.* Feminist Majority Foundation. Retrieved from http://www.womeninpolicing.org/pdf/Fullconsentdecreestudy.pdf
National Center for Women and Policing. (2005). *A history of women in policing in the United States.* Feminist Majority Foundation. Retrieved from http://womeninpolicing.org/history/index.asp
National Research Council. (2004). *Fairness and effectiveness in policing: The evidence.* Washington, DC: National Academies Press.
Ness, C., & Gordon, R. (1995). Beating the rap. *San Francisco Examiner*, A11.
Neugebauer, R. (1999). First nation's people and law enforcement. In M. Corsianos & K.A. Train (Eds.), *Interrogating social justice: Politics, culture and identity* (pp. 247–269). Toronto: Canadian Scholars' Press.
Nichols, D. (1995). The brotherhood: Sexual harassment in police agencies. *Women Police, 29*(2), 10–12.
Orban, C. (1998). Badges, bitches, dykes and whores: Women in the occupation of policing. In S. McMahon (Ed.), *Women, crime and culture: Whores and heroes* (pp. 267–291). Toronto: Centre for Police and Security Studies at York University.
Price, B.R. (1974). A study of leadership strength of female police executives. *Journal of Police Science and Administration, 2*, 219–226.

Prokos, A., & Padavic, I. (2002). 'There oughtta be a law against bitches': Masculinity lessons in police academy training. *Gender, Work, and Organization, 9*, 439–459.
Robinson, G.V. (1993). Sexual harassment in Florida law enforcement: Panacea or Pandora's box. Senior Leadership Research Paper. Retrieved from http://www.fdle.state.fl.us/Content/getdoc/d8578f87-3070-4f10-8d2e-0f57c3766d70/Robinson.aspx
Rosenbaum, D. (Ed.). (1986). *Community crime prevention: Does it work?* Beverly Hills, CA: Sage.
Roth, J.A., Roehl, J., & Johnson, C.C. (2004). Trends in community policing. In W.G. Skogan (Ed.), *Community policing (can it work?)* (pp. 3–29). Belmont, CA: Thomson Wadsworth.
Scheurich, J.J., & Young, M.D. (2002). White racism among white faculty: From critical understanding to antiracist activism. In W.A. Smith, P.G. Altbach, & K. Lomotey (Eds.), *The racial crisis in American higher education: Continuing challenges for the 21st century* (pp. 221–242). New York: SUNY Press.
Schulz, D.M. (2004). Invisible no more: A social history of women in U.S. policing. In B.R. Price & N.J. Sokoloff (Eds.), *The criminal justice system and women: Offenders, prisoners, victims, & workers* (3rd ed.) (pp. 483–494). New York: McGraw-Hill.
Scripture, A.E. (1997). The sources of police culture: Demographic or environmental variables? *Policing and Society, 7*(3), 63–176.
Skogan, W.G. (Ed.). (1990). *Disorder and decline.* New York: Free Press.
Skogan, W.G. (Ed.). (1996). The community's role in community policing. *National Institute of Justice Journal,* 31–34.
Skogan, W.G. (Ed.). (2004). *Community policing (can it work?).* Belmont, CA: Thomson Wadsworth.
Spelman, W., & Eck, J.E. (1987). *Problem-oriented policing.* Washington, DC: National Institute of Justice (Research in Brief Series).
Statistics Canada. (2005). Police personnel and expenditures. *The daily.* Canada: Minister of Industry. Retrieved from http://www.statcan.ca/Daily/English/051215/d051215d.htm
Stenson, K. (1993). Community policing as governmental technology. *Economy and Society, 22*(3), 373–389.
Storch, J., & Panzarella, R. (1996). Police stress: State-trait anxiety in relation to occupational and personal stressors. *Journal of Criminal Justice, 24*(2), 99–107.
Thacher, D. (2001). Conflicting values in community policing. *Law & Society Review, 35*(4), 765–798.
Trojanowicz, R.J. (1983). An evaluation of a neighborhood foot patrol program. *Journal of Police Science and Administration, 11*(4), 410–419.
Trojanowicz, R.J., & Bucqueroux, B. (1990). *Community policing: A contemporary perspective.* Cincinnati, OH: Anderson.
United States Department of Labor. (2007). *Bureau of labor statistics – annual averages: nontraditional occupations for women in 2007.* Washington, DC: US Department of Labor. Retrieved from http://www.dol.gov/wb/factsheets/nontra2007_txt.htm
Van Wormer, K.S., & Bartollas, C. (2000). *Women and the criminal justice system.* Boston, MA: Allyn & Bacon.
Walker, S., & Katz, C.M. (2005). *Police in America: An introduction* (5th ed.). New York: McGraw-Hill.
Wilson, J.Q., & Kelling, G.L. (1982). Broken windows: The police and neighborhood safety. *Atlantic Monthly,* 29–38.
Wyrick, P.A. (2000). *Law enforcement referral of at-risk youth: The SHIELD program.* Washington, DC: Office of Juvenile Justice and Delinquency Prevention, US Department of Justice.
Zdanowicz, M. (2001). A shift in care. *Community Links,* 3–5.
Zhao, J., He, N., & Lovrich, N. (2003). Community policing: Is it changing the basic functions of policing in the 1990s? *Justice Quarterly, 20*, 697–724.

Policing 'below the state' in Germany: neocommunitarian soberness and punitive paternalism

Volker Eick

Department of Social Sciences, Institute for the Analysis of Society and Policy, Goethe Universität Frankfurt am Main, Frankfurt/M., Germany

For the last three decades, community-oriented approaches have been considered to be progressive and adequate ways to address unemployment, poverty, social marginalization, as well as disorder and crime by a plethora of social scientists and practitioners in Europe and North America. During the last decade, respective programs have been institutionalized in Europe and elsewhere. Within a framework known as the 'activating welfare state,' or even 'the activating city' in Germany, nonprofits working in fields such as labor market (re)integration, social stabilization of 'disadvantaged' communities, or crime prevention adopt increasingly ambivalent roles. On the one hand, (local) administrations integrate them into new networks and forms of cooperative governance; on the other hand, they are forced to comply with the new policies regarding long-term unemployed and welfare recipients (Hartz laws) that combine state subsidies with a strict work commitment (workfare) and, thus, have to bear and procure exclusion processes for those unwilling or unable to conform with the new demands. In addition, nonprofits adopt the role of policing entities, thus creating programs that result in 'the poor policing the poor'. Against this background, the paper discusses the German federal program 'Socially Integrative City' and the Hartz laws as neocommunitarian approaches with regard to labor market (re)integration, security, and (dis)order executed by, among others, nonprofits at the local scale. Nonprofits today are part of a community-based system of mobilizing and motivating, tracing and tracking, securing and socially sorting – thus, being at risk (if not willing) to fail in seeking justice for the 'undesirables.' The paper gives empirical evidence from major German cities.

For the last three decades, community- or neighborhood-oriented approaches have been considered to be progressive and adequate ways to address unemployment, poverty, social marginalization, as well as disorder and crime by a plethora of social scientists and practitioners in Europe and North America (for a critical overview, see Mayer, 1994). During the last decade, respective programs have been institutionalized in Europe and elsewhere – aiming at the social stabilization of 'disadvantaged' communities, the integration of different stakeholders into new governance arrangements, the so-called empowerment of the citizenry, and the modernization of the public bureaucracy (Becker, Thomas, Löhr, & Rösner, 2002; IfS, 2004; Mayer, 2009, pp. 7–14). Within a framework known as the 'activating welfare state' (Dingeldey, 2009; Eichhorst, Grienberger-Zingerle, & Konle-Seidl, 2006), or even 'the activating city' (Schulze-Böing, 2000) in Germany, nonprofit organizations working in fields such as labor market (re)integration, social stabilization of 'disadvantaged' communities, or crime prevention are adopting increasingly ambivalent roles.

In the following, I, *firstly*, analyze one of the largest space-based programs in Germany heralded by its proponents as *the* community-oriented and neighborhood program to combat poverty and social exclusion, and to stabilize 'disadvantaged' neighborhoods (BMVBS, 2009; Bundesregierung, 2009; Bundestransferstelle Soziale Stadt, 2008; Häußermann, 2005), the 'Socially Integrative City' program.[1] Established in 1999, it shows how nonprofits gained greater influence not only in terms of broader and deeper governance integration[2] but also in their ability to institutionalize new regimes of cleanliness, order, and security, or in German, *Sicherheit, Ordnung und Sauberkeit* (SOS) on the local scale.[3] From 2005 onwards, nonprofits have also been able to extend their influence due to a new labor market regime.

I, therefore, *secondly*, characterize the current German workfare system as it has been developed from 2002 onwards, peaking in 2005, when the then government of the Social Democrats and the Green Party introduced the so-called Hartz laws (Knuth, 2009; Lavelle, 2007; Mayer, 2009), as an attempt to bring neoliberal policies to the fore. This legislation in particular led to a more intense integration of nonprofit organizations (hereinafter referred to as nonprofits) – in the literature also known as Third Sector organizations (Evers, 1995; Salamon, 2002) – into the 'activating welfare state.' Whereas labor market integration (especially of the 'worst-off') has been a task of nonprofits ever since (Eick, Mayer, Grell, & Sambale, 2004) – including policing of what local governments perceive as a lack of cleanliness, order, and security (Eick, 2008) – they became more aggressively involved into policing issues with the advent of community-oriented programs orchestrated by the local state in the mid-2000s (Eick, 2003).

Thirdly, as the 'Socially Integrative City' (SIC) program vests nonprofits with informal quasi-policing powers on the ground, I give empirical evidence about their practices against their main 'target groups,' homeless people, drug addicts, alcoholics, and – increasingly, since the Hartz laws came into operation – also against the long-term unemployed by forcing them to conform to workfare measures that also relate to SOS services.[4]

What we are witnessing today is a threefold development: *Firstly*, the influence of nonprofits is growing due to laws such as the Hartz IV clauses concentrating on labor market (re)integration of long-term unemployed by workfare measures and in programs tackling cleanliness, order, and security policies (SOS) – labor market integration and SOS programs are even merging; *secondly*, space-oriented programs such as the 'Socially Integrative City' program tend to institutionalize and spatialize the influence of nonprofits within local 'growth coalitions' (Lauria, 1997; Logan & Molotch, 1987) – with exclusionary effects for the most 'disadvantaged'; *thirdly*, since the mid-1990s, nonprofits have become members of the 'extended policing family' (Crawford & Lister, 2004), building coalitions with the state police and rent-a-cops – but they are not only engaged in cooperative coalitions but also aiming at cooptation of and competition with the 'family members' and with each other (Eick, 2008).

The socio-economic restructuring of German cities in ways of 'urban entrepreneurialism' (Harvey, 1989) is embedded in a general long-term trend: the neoliberal reorganization of capitalism in order to enhance competition for profit reasons. This trend can be described, for a start, as *devolution* – the shifting of responsibilities from the national to the local scale; accompanied by an intensified competition on the urban scale between and within cities. In sum, cities are becoming more entrepreneurial. As Swyngedouw (1997) has shown, the global and the local are interlinked in a process of 'glocalization,' through which occurs the simultaneous shifting of regulatory tasks (and the creation of corresponding institutions) from the national scale to supranational and local scales.[5] Related to these processes are, as Mayer (2007, p. 91) states, new forms of urban governance:

> Cities are today confronting a more competitive (global) environment, and local governments have taken to place marketing, enterprise zones, tax abatements, public–private partnerships, and new forms of local boosterism ... Urban forms of governance have become entrepreneurialized, emphasizing economic efficiency, low taxes, individual responsibility, and user fees; the most important goal of urban policy has become to mobilize city space as an arena for market-oriented economic growth.

Further, urban entrepreneurialism creates what can be called 'monied oligarchies' in an 'informal constitutional state,' or *informeller Rechtsstaat* (Bohne, 1981) on the local scale. From this perspective, the SIC program can not only be understood as a form of devolution but also as a particular form of the institutionalization of lobbyism coordinated by local urban regimes (Lauria, 1997) as will be shown in the next section. *Finally*, and by the same token, the relatively centralized – in comparison to other larger OECD countries – German Public Employment Service (PES) underwent a decentralization strategy, thus mirroring one of the SIC program's core understandings that local problems should be addressed on the local scale.

The 'Socially Integrative City': the duty to become empowered

The urban development program 'Socially Integrative City' (SIC) was launched in 1999 by the Federal Ministry of Transport, Building and Urban Affairs (BMVBS). According to its own account (BMVBS, 2009), the program aims to counteract growing socio-spatial polarization in German cities and upgrade and stabilize deprived neighborhoods. In addition to investing in the renovation and redevelopment of buildings and the living environment, the program seeks to improve the living situation of neighborhood residents. In the period between 1999 and 2007, some 500 neighborhoods in around 320 cities and communities were allocated funding of more than €2 billion.[6] Each year, some 50 new neighborhoods become program areas. In addition, supplementary labor market (re)integration programs are being implemented in the program areas (Becker et al., 2002; BMVBS, 2009; Bundestransferstelle Soziale Stadt, 2008; Lauff, 2010).

The program works on the premise of strong area-based, socio-spatial orientation and active resident participation, and thus is more explicit about a spatial focus compared to the Hartz laws that introduced workfare in Germany in 2005 (see below); nevertheless, agreements exist between the PES and local stakeholders (the district administrations, the neighborhood managers) that Hartz IV subsidies and other labor market funding should be concentrated in the SIC program's areas, also known as neighborhood management areas (Bundestransferstelle Soziale Stadt, 2008). Additionally, the SIC program requires not only that the nonprofits participate but moreover that they take lead positions – as they are to run the program together with the neighborhood managers and thus, in line with Osborne and Gaebler's (1992, pp. 25, 49) notions of 'steering rather than rowing' and 'empowering rather than serving,' the (nation) state creates a new governance regime. Furthermore, the new governance model includes the involvement of commercial 'stakeholders' such as local business communities, local public institutions such as schools, community-based and grassroots organizations, plus – and at the same time as the main target group – (disadvantaged) residents: The so-called 'empowerment' of the urban poor is a keyword in both the Hartz laws (where they are called 'main target audience') and the 'Socially Integrative City' program (where they are called 'disadvantaged segments of the population'),[7] and it is heavily loaded with an ideology of duty, thus a moralization of politics more generally. Since the aim of the SIC program is not to fight the causes of poverty (Becker et al., 2002; Häußermann & Kapphan, 2000; Mayer, 2009) offering neither meaningful subsidies nor decent jobs for the urban poor, let alone higher or rising earnings (Eick, 2008), such 'Keynesian' incentives have been replaced by a rhetoric of duty and self-responsibility (Ehrke, 1999).

Experimenting in the urban laboratory

Such programs – the 'New Deal for Communities' in the UK would be just another example (Lawless, 2006; Wallace, 2007) – represent varieties of experimentation within urban environments. From the late 1990s onwards, cities became what Brenner and Theodore (2002, p. 21) called 'important geographical targets and institutional laboratories' for a variety of policy experiments to address consequences of neoliberalism such as poverty and social exclusion. These policy experiments have taken different forms in different places in ways that, as Jessop (2002) outlines, include neostatist, neocorporatist, and, important for the strategies of the aforementioned nonprofits, neocommunitarianist experiments.

Under neoliberalism, diverse tasks of government are removed from the (national) state bureaucracy and dispersed throughout various local administrations and agencies (devolution), be they commercial enterprises, philanthropic organizations, nonprofits, or groups of citizens (Eick et al., 2004; Eisenschitz & Gough, 1996; Giddens, 1998; Novy & Hammer, 2007). The community as a means of government (Rose, 1996), or what Ilcan and Basok (2004) call 'community government,' has become an ever expanding political project wherein target communities have been identified by political reformers and their academic allies as either potential sites of virtue, democracy, and efficiency (Etzioni, 1996; Evers, 1995; Fyfe, 2005), or as socio-spatial entities with a lack thereof, and thus, according to its proponents, in need of intervention in an even more paternalistic manner (Becker et al., 2002; Eick, 2009; Lanz, 2000; Lavelle, 2007). From a German perspective, the current labor market (re)integration and neighborhood policies exhibit a neoliberal economic sensibility camouflaged in the legitimating rhetoric of neocommunitarianism (Eick, 2008; cf. Boudreau, Hamel, Jouve, & Keil, 2006; Márquez & Pérez, 2008).[8]

Paternalistic neocommunitarianism

The underlying concept of such a political project is a particular understanding of neocommunitarianism. Neocommunitarianism is the way, in which the contemporary proponents of the current processes of labor market (re)integration and social stabilization of localities define, shape, and orient 'communities' (e.g. in 'disadvantaged' neighborhoods) and target groups (e.g. long-term unemployed) in such a way that these proponents engage in activities that attempt to make certain groups of citizens and/or even themselves responsible for particular purposes and ends (Tam, 1998; Tok 2009). According to McCarthy (2005), neocommunitarianism reinvents market liberalism within outwardly compassionate institutions which champion community affairs, but with a clandestine extension of market processes to new spheres.

On the one hand, the neocommunitarian logic encourages processes of 'community' building, aims at overcoming the anonymity between individuals and, implicitly, favors and even creates communities that are said to share desirable common understandings, behaviors, and experiences, namely the inner-city middle class (Rose, 1996). On the other hand, (local) administrations and nonprofits pursue a neocommunitarian social order within which unemployment is constructed as an *individual guilt*, work is perceived as a *sine qua non duty*, and a 'non-conformist' lifestyle such as public drinking (not to be mingled with binge drinking, or alcoholism among teenagers) is denounced as undermining social cohesion. In that sense, the urban poor – those who cannot afford, or are not willing to drink in bars, restaurants, or, say, the *Oktoberfest* – are the direct targets of such paternalistic programs. In other words and as another example, those long-term unemployed being unable to reintegrate themselves into the labor market are perceived economically as 'investment ruins,' socially as 'parasites' (for an early analysis, see Spitzer, 1975).

It is here where nonprofits play a decisive role, and, for the purpose of clarification, it is useful to briefly characterize them as not only beyond the spheres of state, economy, and 'civil society' (family, informal economy) but also to touch on the diversity within the sector.

Nonprofits: from stakeholders to shareholders?

'Nonprofit organization' is an ill-defined term (Martens, 2002; Morris, 2000). For the purpose of this paper, it should be good enough to clarify that nonprofits are organizationally independent from the state and from for-profit business; are formally structured, have a legally fixed constitution, lack a profit-maximizing orientation, rely on voluntary contributions, and, by legal definition, should work in the public interest and serve the commonweal, i.e. to be *gemeinnützig* (Anheier & Seibel, 1993; Eick et al., 2004; Salamon, 2002). They are perceived as those stakeholders best suited to fill the gaps that either the state (neglecting particular parts of the population) or the economy (unable to identify meaningful profit options) leave behind. Based on this understanding two groups of nonprofits can be identified.

In Berlin, for example, out of 1500 nonprofits, around 100 are called 'labor market-oriented employment providers' by the labor administration and (until December 2009) received additional public funding to (re)integrate the (long-term) unemployed into the labor market.[9] In Hamburg, out of 1000 nonprofits it is just one large agency that is in charge of long-term unemployed (Eick, 2009; cf. Briken & Eick, 2011). In a nutshell, the majority of nonprofits is not providing services for the state and just runs their ordinary businesses such as providing child care, operating a neighborhood center or a soup kitchen; they might get subsidies from the state, though.[10] For the others – the 100-something in Berlin and the one nonprofit in Hamburg with an additional dozen of common-or-garden supporting organizations – the long-term unemployed *are* the business. Service-providing nonprofits would, for example, develop a labor market integration project, submit their proposals, including a financial plan, to the PES or JobCenter, coordinate with the local administrations and, if successful, would get the monies necessary to run the work (re)integration project. For their attempt to (re)integrate the unemployed they will be provided with a lump sum; the amount being particularly high for long-term unemployed.[11]

Whatever the mainstream literature suggests, in contrast to the often romanticized understanding of nonprofits as small and tidy do-gooders – and here, focusing on those nonprofits that are into labor market (re)integration – they form (inter)national networks of highly professionalized service providers better characterized as an '(un)employment industry' with significant importance when it comes to policy enforcement. Even though nonprofits, by law and definition, are not allowed to generate profits[12] for private purposes, they nevertheless create significant turnovers.

Importantly, nonprofits have been integrated into the local welfare state as service providers since the mid-1980s. Many of them emerged from the new social movements of the 1970s and early 1980s; still, they are community-based in the sense that they have particular local knowledge about the respective neighborhoods, where they emerged, are still based, and/or are working. They professionalized their services in the years that followed; eventually, they became integrated into the local welfare state, providing services under the auspices of the public labor market administration, the PES, and the district bureaucracy. The Hartz laws intensified not only the cooperation with but the cooptation of nonprofits by the state apparatus (Kotlenga, 2008) but also offered them new opportunities as experts for local affairs (Eick, 2008).

Today, they play *the* decisive role in implementing this new workfare system as it is the nonprofits that invent and introduce, develop and design, organize and oversee the new compulsory work measures (Eick et al., 2004, pp. 56–64). The notion that nonprofits are 'pursuing charitable purposes rather than private profits' and 'are committed to "the cause," rather than merely to maximizing profits or managerial efficiency' (Goodin, 2003, p. 372) is naive, or, at least, contestable. Empirical evidence shows that, even though in a variety of ways, nonprofits are incorporated, and are willing to incorporate themselves, into the respective hierarchical concepts of workfare and subordination (Eick et al., 2004; Fritsche, 2003; Kotlenga, 2008; Leitner, Peck, & Sheppard, 2007; Mayer, 2009), and thus execute a top-down profitable plus punitive paternalism. In working for the state and the employment offices for gain, they literally turn from stakeholders into shareholders. One of their tasks is, in the broadest sense, to create and up-value neighborhoods and to increase certain values within the communities.

Creating and upgrading communities

In order to do so, the respective residents are hence to be 'empowered,' 'activated,' and contained or, where perceived as necessary, to be replaced (Scraton, 2004; Spitzer, 1975). Spitzer (1975, p. 645) distinguishes between 'a costly yet relatively harmless burden to society,' the 'social junk,' and potential trouble-makers that tend 'to be more youthful, alienated, and political volatile' (1975, p. 646), the 'social dynamite,' and clarifies – with intriguing clarity – that 'social dynamite is normally processed through the legal system with its capacity for active intervention, while social junk is frequently (but not always) administered by the agencies and agents of the therapeutic and welfare state' (1975, p. 646). While one today would talk about the *workfare state* instead of the welfare state, what can be observed today (for empirical evidence, see below) is that potential troublemakers are

> Recruited as policemen, social workers and attendants, while confirmed deviants can be 'rehabilitated' by becoming counselors, psychiatric aides and parole officers. In other

> words, if a large number of the controlled can be converted into a first line of defense, threats to the system of class rule can be transformed into resources for its support. (Spitzer, 1975, p. 649)[13]

With all due rosy-tinted social romanticism in the SIC program's lyric and with all the soberness of the rhetoric of law,[14] a pro-growth upgrading of the 'disadvantaged' quarters is part and parcel of the program (Eick, 2009; Frank, 2005). One way to do so is by changing the perceptions of the residents by creating feelings of 'us' and 'them' (Márquez & Pérez, 2008).

Following Rose, the neighborhood management and the SIC program as a whole can be described as a particular form of community governance as such programs:

> attempt to 'empower' the inhabitants of particular inner-city locales by constituting those who reside in a certain locality *as* 'a' community, by seeking out 'community groups' who can claim to speak 'in the name of community' and by linking them in new ways into the political apparatus in order to enact programs which seek to regenerate the economic and human fabric of an area. (1996, p. 336, emphasis in original)

In essence, such a desire for a 'purified community' appears on the one hand to point to the fear of diversity and seems to be an apology for homogeneity (Márquez & Pérez, 2008). On the other hand, the interplay of a neoliberal ethos, which heralds individual freedom and individual choice (instead of collective solidarity), promotes *Chancen-gerechtigkeit* instead of *Chancengleichheit* (equity of chances instead of equality of chances), and sends the age-old message to the urban poor that they should 'accept their material disadvantages and seek a form of secondary gratification in doing their duty' (Ehrke, 1999, p. 10). Thus, such new local governance regimes are best understood as a (last) offer-you-cannot-refuse to the 'disadvantaged' to pull themselves up from the morass of (self-inflicted) poverty and dependency by their own bootstraps. The mission issued to the professionalized nonprofits by the state – to stabilize the social situation within the 'disadvantaged' quarters by empowering the residents; to encourage an overarching resort and institutional cooperative approach; and to accelerate the modernization of the public administrations (Senat von Berlin, 2008) – can thus be characterized as an attempt of the (local) state to establish a 'civil society from above' (Lanz, 2000). Finally, in trying to cushion the – well spotted but systematically de-thematized – neoliberal economic, social, and cultural forms of exclusion on the local scale, neighborhood management likewise is an enforcing instrument and flanking mechanism to assert and safeguard the dismantling of the welfare state (Eisenschitz & Gough, 1996; Krummacher, Kulbach, Waltz, & Wohlfahrt, 2003). Notwithstanding the existence of nonprofits that aim to resist or, at least try to mend the worst excesses of neoliberalism on the local scale (Eick et al., 2004, pp. 132–143; Goodin, 2003; Kotlenga, 2008), it is to those nonprofits being at risk (if not willing) to fail in seeking justice for the urban poor in the fields of local social politics (SIC program) and labor market (re)integration (Hartz IV) the paper is focused on. Before giving empirical evidence, the paper first turns to the Hartz legislation in more detail.

The German Hartz Laws: workfare meets neoliberal neighborhoods

In the autumn of 2003, the Red–Green federal coalition passed a package of measures, dubbed Agenda 2010. The Agenda comprised the standard ingredients Jessop (2002) and others (Brenner, Jessop, Jones, & MacLeod, 2003; Brenner & Theodore, 2002; Leitner et al., 2007) characterize as 'actually existing neoliberalism': cutting the dole, raising the age of retirement, outsourcing health-insurance, reducing subsidies, abolishing craft requirements, extending shopping hours; in sum, the German Social-Democracy had 'steeled itself to the social retrenchment and deregulation of the labor market from which Christian Democracy, throughout its long years in power, had flinched' (Anderson, 2009, p. 8).

One part of the Agenda 2010 package is the so-called Hartz I–IV laws. Whereas Hartz I–III comprise new activating programs, tighter definitions of suitable work, a more flexible sanction regime, and the internal reorganization of the PES structure,[15] Hartz IV covers the reform of the unemployment benefit and social assistance system (Hans Böckler Stiftung, 2006). As for the latter, social insurance is now exclusively restricted to the short-term unemployed, whereas long-term unemployed people only have access to basic social assistance (€359 per month, plus heating and rent) – even for low-wage workers these €359 mark a drastic decline after 12 months of unemployment (18 months for those older than 55 years) compared to the old system that allowed for an open-ended and means-tested replacement of the former income by 53% (for single persons) and 57% (for persons with children).[16] In sum, Hartz IV ended the insurance-type principles of social protection; introduced the obligation to take any job regardless of the wage level and one's qualification,[17] thus, the long-term unemployed are forced into any kind of workfare measures (for a more detailed, even though somewhat idealistic, overview of Hartz IV, see Knuth, 2009; on workfare in general, see Peck, 2001). Just as Giddens (1998, p. 65) formulated the motto for the 'Third Way' in the UK, 'no rights without responsibilities,' the German workfare system translates its own new program into the slogan *Fördern und Fordern* (supporting and stipulating) as the key principle of the new approach to labor market (re)integration.

One-Euro-jobs: the new cash cow for nonprofits

Part and parcel of the new workfare measures under Hartz IV are the so-called 'one-Euro-jobs' – employment relationships for long-term unemployed that are not subject to social insurance contributions; are not labor contracts but just allowances; only allow for jobs that are paid between one and two and a half Euros per hour; and that, according to the labor law, have to be additional, or *zusätzlich* (i.e. they should not lead to the replacement of regular workers who have the same position with – if at all – tariff wages);[18] they should be in the public interest and serve the public good (*gemeinnützig*). In practice though,

> The new one-Euro-jobs provided for in Hartz IV have already broken down [the] wall and contribute to the creation of a low-wage (subsidized) labor market, replacing regular workers especially in the social service sector and in the janitorial business with workfare workers. (Mayer, 2009, p. 28; cf. ver.di 2007)

In order to – at least officially – avoid the replacement of regular employment by one-Euro-jobs, nonprofits 'create' so-called niche occupations,[19] including work opportunities in health care, eldercare, education, and in the aforementioned SOS field, i.e. cleanliness, order, and security, where long-term unemployed are deployed as (additional) street cleaners, wardens, 'tourist ambassadors,' security guards, and the like (Eick, 2003; Helms, 2008); the security guards accounting for up to 15% of all one-Euro-jobs in cities such as Hamburg and Berlin (Briken & Eick, 2011; Eick, 2009).

As nonprofits are neither autonomous from state and market logics nor by any means unwavering against the demands of their employers – the local administrations and the PES – their attitudes toward their 'clients' and toward the new workfare environment change. Additionally, nonprofits working within the 'market' of labor (re)integration are heterogeneous actors and even these differences are made marketable; therefore, being shaped by and shaping their respective environs – in the case at hand, shaped by workfare strategies under 'actually existing neoliberalism' (Brenner & Theodore, 2002) as well as shaping the introduction and implementation of the various neoliberal workfare strategies (England & Ward, 2007; Leitner et al., 2007; Smith, Stenning, & Willis, 2008).

As the case studies below show, many nonprofits act in ways that allow for the implementation of workfare strategies and authoritarian control measures in smoother and less confrontational manners (Eick et al., 2004, pp. 151–184; cf. Fyfe, 2005; Lake & Newman, 2002; Smith, 1998), or, as other examples illustrate, even more confrontational (Eick, 2009).

Even though the implementation of the Hartz reform was meant to be and indeed is more space-based – in particular, in the more than 2100 SIC program areas (Bundesregierung, 2009, p. 41) – compared to the earlier work (re)integration programs of the 1990s, the main focus of the PES with its 10 regional directorates and 180 local PES offices is still on *persons* and less so on *spaces*.[20] Nevertheless, the 346 JobCenters are focused in particular on the hard(est) to employ[21] and include spaces dubbed as 'failing' or 'failed communities' in their considerations. In February 2010 the Berlin JobCenter responsible for the district of Neukölln moved its headquarter directly into the 'failing community,' and at the same time SIC program area, Rollberg-Viertel (Schmiemann, 2010), and already in January of the same year started a model project in the Highdeck-Siedlung.[22] In these neighborhoods, described as both 'disadvantaged' and 'disadvantaging,' allegedly suffering from a 'cumulative self-intensifying downward spiral' of social segregation (Häußermann & Kapphan, 2000, pp. 229–234), nonprofits deploy their workfare measures.

From both programs, the SIC program and the Hartz laws, nonprofits benefit in many ways: from autonomous program implementation to decisive decision-making; from extended income opportunities to the power of defining what is to be understood as 'acceptable' behavior within the 'disadvantaged' areas and among the long-term unemployed. It is to this 'power of naming' (Dworkin, 1981) and the respective abilities to enforce what these nonprofits perceive as the duties of the 'disadvantaged' the paper now turns.

Shock and awe: labor market virtues within the 'activating city'

In recent years, service-providing nonprofits dovetailed labor market (re)integration of long-term unemployed with local SOS policies in a more intense manner and, in doing so, extended their sphere of action. They started to do policing 'below the state' and thus were able to outcompete possible rivals from both the state and commercial sphere, at least in the SIC areas.[23] In addition, given a stricter focus on workfare, activation, empowerment and employability, labor market-oriented nonprofits have also been able to oust other nonprofits. The new horizontal and vertical integration allowed them to extend their influence in the now relevant networks (and thus, the respective local regimes) and, even more important, to assert new understandings of 'cooperation' under the SIC program.[24]

Nonprofits, active as neighborhood managers within the SIC program, are also involved in employability programs, in particular for youths. According to several sources, some nonprofits translate work placement and the testing of work readiness into 'shock and awe' measures that either lead to meaningless training measures, working poor jobs, or disqualification for unemployment benefits (Berliner Kampagne, 2008; Gern & Segbers, 2009; ver.di, 2007):

> The precondition for work placement consultancy, the nonprofit representative explained, 'is the appearance of the applicant with full-fledged documents … and appropriate clothing. This already deters around 50% of all applicants.' according to the nonprofit officer. The main function of the work placement consultancy, she continues, is lifestyle regulation 'that is to be achieved by confronting the juvenile with labor market virtues such as punctuality, cleanliness, and reliability.' (cited in Fritsche, 2003, pp. 86–87)

As mentioned above, nonprofits together with the public employment offices, the JobCenters, the district administrations, and neighborhood managers are actively pursuing workfare measures. The public administrations are mainly overseeing finance and bureaucracy and the neighborhood managers rarely run labor market programs. It is the roughly 100 nonprofits in Berlin, specialized in labor market (re)integration, that are key for the implementation of the Hartz IV workfare measures and the respective responsibilization of the unemployed. An academic supporter of the new system, in order to safeguard the compliance of the unemployed, clarified the last point and claimed it to be necessary 'to make the client understand, in any available form, the precarious financial situation of the municipality by tackling her everyday life directly' (Schulze-Böing, 2000, p. 54).

Several elements are therefore vital for the effective implementation and enforcement of the new workfare regime, the overall concept of 'the activating state' and most notably the 'activating city.' *Firstly*, the regional JobCenters are setting the legal framework for the coercive measures to be deployed against the long-term unemployed and, where need be, they readjust the rulings.[25] On the ground though, *secondly*, it is the nonprofits that enforce the regulations, provide the supposedly additional jobs, and report about noncompliance of the unemployed, now called 'customers.' *Finally*, together with the district administration and the respective state departments, all stakeholders involved form a growth coalition and identify themselves as the 'labor market family' (Eick et al., 2004).[26] Aside from such family 'psychobabble' (Forsyth, 2008), it is noteworthy that the nonprofits are the only ones that directly generate an income from the coalition. Given the sheer number of unemployed being 'mobilized,' some observers describe the labor market-oriented nonprofits, the PES, and the JobCenter rightly as an 'employment industry,' or 'poverty industry' (Müller, 2009; ver.di, 2007). While squeezing profits out of their 'customers,' nonprofits leave them without any meaningful perspective on the labor market, help to create a low-wage sector, and even participate in weakening the benefits and rights of regular workers (Klute, 2008). It is this peculiarity of the customer-orientation deployed by nonprofits within the field of labor market (re)integration that the paper will now address.

Multiple labor and security markets: 'customer-orientation' of a peculiar kind

The following sections will provide empirical evidence for the fact that – flanked with the devolution within the urban growth regimes on the local scale, fuelled by the SIC program and Hartz IV, allowed for by the institutionalization of lobbyism (Bohne, 1981), and by the decentralization of administrative structures – labor market-oriented nonprofits managed to develop, implement, and deploy a policing strategy 'below and beyond' the state.

One of the service-providing nonprofits is BEQUIT (Employment and Qualification Company Tempelhof). With salaried personnel of 20 in 2008, the company mobilized hundreds of long-term unemployed and generated an annual turnover of about €7 million or US $9.7 million (Eick, 2009, p. 306). With blanket coverage BEQUIT shapes the SIC program in the Berlin district of Neukölln and is the oligopolist if it comes to cleanliness, order, and security. Under the headline 'supervision projects of BEQUIT,' long-term unemployed are engaged as school and schoolyard attendants, as school-way escorts, as park inspectors, as supervisors of residential areas and playgrounds – in the quarter Schillerpromenade alone, 24 long-term unemployed undertake such tasks as one-Euro-jobbers for a population of just 20,000 (Hömberg, 2007); in addition, according to BEQUIT's website, they 'control underground parking lots, enforce public green space by-laws, and are available as contact persons in emergency and conflict situations, and pay heed to cleanliness.'[27] A similar project, launched in 2005, had already attracted nationwide attention because of the sheer number of one-Euro-jobbers: Since then, 350 long-term unemployed control all playgrounds (ca. 120) in the district of Neukölln as so-called 'Spielplatzkümmerer,' or playground attendants (Fuchs, 2005; ver.di, 2007, pp. 17–18). In order to defend nonprofits against accusations by the service union *Vereinte Dienstleistungsgewerkschaft* (ver.di) that jobs on the regular labor market are substituted by one-Euro-jobbers, a representative tackled this tender point with this telling answer:

> The easiest way to describe their duties is to clarify what [the one-Euro-jobbers] are not – namely police officers, trash collectors, or swing repairmen. Instead, it's their task, alone with their presence, to bar potential 'play ground disturbers' from drinking alcohol, to throw garbage in the sandbox and to rampage. (cited in Leber, 2005, p. 9, emphasis in original)

Such comments show in all clarity how much nonprofits are aware about the resulting crowding out of regular jobs by their one-Euro-job workfare measures while in parallel, implicitly purporting to be *the* policing force against the urban poor.

While BEQUIT developed itself as *the* expert for nonprofit policing in the SIC program's areas, especially in the district of Neukölln where it holds an oligopoly,[28] the same can be said about another nonprofit, Neuraum (new space), as it runs 11 concierge boxes with 38 long-term unemployed, thus being the market leader in this field of expertise in Berlin. According to one representative, the nonprofit 'realizes the concierge concept in cooperation with large housing societies at social hotspots' (Schmid, 2006, p. 9). It is financed by the public employment offices, the JobCenter, and the European Social Fund.[29] Since 2000, one-Euro-jobbers do 'circuits within the buildings and in the outside sections; are to mediate in conflict situations ... and cooperate with caretakers, housing companies, the police, and youth welfare centers.'[30]

As the SIC program claims to be integrative, the question arises: what does such an 'integrative' approach mean for the urban poor in practical terms? In Berlin's district of Wedding, for example, the police banned alcoholics from the area by request of the neighborhood management; the district administration removed street furniture; and 'all pergolas and raised beds' were removed. 'Now, there are no more hiding spaces for alcoholics, they will never feel comfortable here again,' the neighborhood manager rejoiced in an interview (cited in Schuster, 2003, p. 12). In the district of Prenzlauer Berg, the neighborhood management reacted in the same way, cleared the area of alcoholics, and even classified the drunkards into the 'categories of a local and trans-local drinker milieu' (Holm, 2001, p. 9).

The most current and quite aggressive move is under way in the aforementioned SIC program area Schillerpromenade where a so-called 'Task Force Okerstraße' has been established:

> Since 2005, the number of complaints voiced by residents about the annoyances emanating from the drinkers at the Schillerpromenade increased. Besides the problems with these carousers ... [at the Okerstraße,] neighborhood conflicts are mounting due to unattended, partway ill-kept kids and adolescents predominantly stemming from Roman families ... A totally new major problem derives from the eastward EU enlargement since 2007, leading, predominantly in the summer months, to an enormous surge of 'seasonal workers' primarily from Rumania. Occupancies of two-room apartments with up to eleven persons, black labor and illegal businesses are well-known. (Schmiedeknecht, 2009, p. 2)

The 'Task Force' calls for action by the police and other stakeholders to coordinately fight drinking in neighborhood public spaces (even though public drinking is not prohibited) and, in essence, to get rid of the Roma people stemming from Romania.[31] Just as a reminder: the cited neighborhood managers are employers within a program called 'Socially Integrative City' that claims to be exactly that: social and integrative. Indeed, it is arguable that – similar to the exclusion of segments of the population – *new* communities are (to be) formed by the neighborhood management. Consequently, the Task Force paper designates 'as the *strategic aim* of the [Task Force] project to organize ... the neighborhood anew' (Schmiedeknecht, 2009, p. 4, emphasis in original). Thereby, the neighborhood management needs to '*newly* develop the potential for citizens' involvement' and has to secure the 'creation of a *new* culture of participation and activation, plus to safeguard support for committed inhabitants who struggle for a better residential environment' (Schmiedeknecht, 2009, 12, emphasis added). The same aim is shared by the Federal Ministry of Transport, Building and Urban Affairs which, in its 'Status Report 2008' on the SIC program's progress, stated that 'activation and participation of the local residents will play an even more important role in the future' (Bundestransferstelle Soziale Stadt, 2008, p. 94).

Consultation of the websites run by the Berlin neighborhood managers under the SIC program revealed that about 15 nonprofits are busy with the provision of security and order services. The nonprofit Forum Arbeit & Projekte (forum work & projects), for example, competes with the Bielefeld-based private security company Germania that protects elementary and secondary schools in the Berlin district of Neukölln (Jacobs, 2008; Vogelsang, 2010). In addition, Forum Arbeit & Projekte protects elementary schools in five other Berlin districts.[32] All in all, about 900 long-term unemployed Berliners do nonprofit policing in one-Euro-jobs. In Hamburg, almost 11,500 long-term unemployed worked in one-Euro-jobs out of which 1100 (9.5%) took over duties and responsibilities in cleaning streets and parks, and an additional 1000 (8.5%) were responsible for 'security & order' in 2006 (Freie und Hansestadt Hamburg, 2006, p. 27).[33] Such SOS measures are by far not only a phenomenon in metropolises but also are a comprehensive trend all over Germany.[34]

Unfortunately, there are no nationwide data available, and local reports or even analysis, as far as apparent, are by and large missing. The reasons for this void are obvious, if we are to believe the respective administrations,[35] and, to put it in a nutshell, relate to the complexity such a data collection necessitates and, therefore to the costs; furthermore, neither the government nor the PES are really interested in revealing very detailed facts about the already highly contested Hartz IV reforms if it comes to the question: what *exactly* the one-Euro-jobbers are doing?[36] By the same token, to collect and analyze reliable data on the share of one-Euro-jobs in the local provision of SOS services is barely feasible, as overall little is known about the *specific* activities executed by the one-Euro-jobbers. Nevertheless, this glimpse reveals some of the current developments within the 'extended policing family' (Crawford & Lister, 2004) and allows for some conclusions.

Conclusions: nonprofit policing below (and beyond) the state

What evolves – in the blossoming field of policing – are multiple security markets which, depending on the geographical or social 'tailoring,' develop into, one could say, 'user-specific' forms of risk-management. According to the respective 'security challenges' identified, military, state police, rent-a-cops, and/or nonprofits are deployed in more the less elaborated forms of cooperation, cooptation, and/or competition (Crawford & Lister, 2004; Dubber & Valverde, 2008; Eick, 2007; Henry & Smith, 2007; Jones & Newburn, 2007; Wood & Dupont, 2006).

For the time being, nonprofit policing mainly takes place in 'disadvantaged' areas. The (local) urban elites, it seems, have in all soberness 'pragmatically' agreed on an SOS management in a neocommunitarian line of thinking that aims to foster a model of 'the poor policing the poor' (Eick, 2003) to *the* backbone concept of such local regulatory policies. And, from the perspective of the stakeholders involved, vested interests can be easily identified. The nation state (and its institutional apparatus) devolved their then 'messing around' with the structural reasons for poverty, a direct outcome of the neoliberal politics, for clear motives: From the nation state's point of view, a meaningful preoccupation with poverty hinders its global competitive capacity – consequently, 'the management of misery' has been devolved to the local scale.[37]

Structural adjustments of socio-economic hardship are also not the business of the local state. Instead, on the local scale and within a new framework of coalition-building, networking, and governance, local administrations have a stomach for eliciting, examining, and experimenting with neocommunitarian approaches in their growth coalitions. For local administrations the new governance arrangements make for a chance to more successfully compete with other districts and get rid of the 'undeserving' poor through 'successful' growth on the local scale. In addition, the local state hopes for a greater independence from the national and *Länder* scale in order to become more flexible and competitive.

That is where nonprofits seize the opportunity and profit(eer) from the devastations of neoliberalism in deploying one-Euro-jobs for (and against) long-term unemployed in safety, order, and security measures. Even though programs are given names like 'Socially Integrative City,' not even the potential to meet social and integrative desires, to widen citizens' ability to gain access to well-being and justice can be taken for granted. Already, social justice, to name just one concept, has been re-defined from equity of chances to equality of chances. The policing strategies of nonprofits are seriously undermining integrative approaches further. Nonprofits are aiming here at a policing – far beyond policing 'below the (nation) state,' but, *nota bene*, even beyond democratic accountability, meaningful open debates, and equal rights.

In that sense, what we are witnessing today is the institutionalization of lobbyism by the creation of two programs on the local scale: SIC and Hartz IV. The neocommunitarian mainstream members – the 'labor market family' and the 'neighborhood management family' – are building growth coalitions on the ground while, within them, nonprofits enjoy a particular freedom to deploy what they deem to be necessary to create new 'deserving communities.' Thus, policing nonprofit style develops not only below and beyond the state and creates new policing entities – but even serves as a tool to form 'respectable families,' 'new communities' in order combat the 'undeserving' poor in what is perceived as an 'urban jungle.'

Notes

1. The official title of the program is *Soziale Stadt – Stadtteile mit besonderem Entwicklungsbedarf* (SIC – neighborhoods with a particular need for renewal).
2. Broader (or horizontal) and deeper (or hierarchical) integration are both modes of governance that enhance the influx of nonprofits; they are not only integrated, for example, into public (federal) decision-making bodies but also form (institutionalized) networks, thematic groups, or even conglomerates (Eick et al., 2004; Goodin, 2003).
3. Scale is a produced societal metric that differentiates space. The production of scale is integral to the production of space: 'it can be argued that the current period of global restructuring is marked by particularly profound transformations of scalar organization. Throughout the last two decades, the geoeconomic project of neoliberalism has entailed a massive assault upon established scales of sociopolitical regulation (particularly those of the Keynesian welfare national state) and an aggressive attempt to forge new global, national, regional and local scalar hierarchies in which unrestricted capital mobility, unfettered market relations, intensified commodification, and a logic of "beggar-thy-neighbor" competition are to be permanently institutionalized ... At the same time, however, oppositional movements which strive to block or to roll back the contemporary neoliberal onslaught have likewise begun to mobilize geographical scale in strategic, often highly creative ways' (Brenner, 2001, p. 594; cf. Jessop, Brenner, & Jones, 2008).
4. I would like to thank Kendra Briken, Richard Milgrom, and the two anonymous reviewers for helpful and valuable comments. The final responsibility is of course the author's alone as the usual disclaimers apply.
5. Peck and Tickell (2002) differentiate further and identify an initial phase of *proto*-neoliberalism when cities became flashpoints for major economic dislocations and struggles; an era of *roll-back* neoliberalism in the 1980s when municipalities introduced a variety of cost-cutting measures and privatization of infrastructural facilities; and the phase of *roll-out* neoliberalism which, since the 1990s, has responded to the contradictions of the earlier zero-sum form of entrepreneurialism.
6. The federal government finances one-third of the program's costs; the *Länder* and municipalities bear the remaining two-thirds.
7. Keys to the implementation of the 'Socially Integrative City' program are 'the strategic approaches of personnel and financial resource pooling, empowerment, and participation, as well as the creation of suitable organizational structures, required in city government and in neighborhoods. The framework for this comprises a clear area based focus and the resulting integrated development concepts' (BMVBS, 2008, p. 6).
8. Márquez and Pérez (2008, p. 1466) note that neocommunitarianism is generally understood 'as a search for more agreeable surroundings within which people seek to recover a feeling of community.'
9. Since 2010, these additional monies are distributed among all nonprofits providing labor market (re)integration to allow for a more 'democratic' integration system (personal conversation in February 2010).
10. Some nonprofits might need long-term unemployed as aides in order to run their business – such as an off-culture theatre, a self-organized library, a health center; grassroots organizations might 'hire' somebody to run the office, and so forth – about 100 labor market-oriented nonprofits would facilitate them with such labor force.
11. Under Hartz IV, for example, nonprofits get a lump sum of about 400 Euros per capita to pay the one-Euro-jobs and to train the long-term unemployed (20% of each labor market integration measure should be reserved for training): the cheaper the training can be provided, the higher the profit.

12. Any kinds of profits are to be reinvested in the nonprofit's stated purpose and cannot be used for investments in other fields of activity or kept for private purposes (Eick et al., 2004).
13. Indeed, the Berlin Senate hired former gang-bangers as a nonprofit policing force, the so-called *Kiezläufer* (neighborhood runners) for a *very* particular neighborhood (Berlin-Kreuzberg), already in 2007 (Deggerich, 2007).
14. The Federal Building Code states in §171e, 'activities of town planning within the social city program are activities to stabilize and up-value ... disadvantaged city districts' (Baugesetzbuch, 2004, p. 93). The Berlin Senate describes as the aim of the program, 'to upgrade the neighborhood, better the attractiveness of the location and the image of the quarter' (Senat von Berlin, 2008, p. 65).
15. To highlight the shift to a more management-oriented reorganization of the German PES, the Federal Institute for Employment (*Bundesanstalt für Arbeit*) was renamed to Federal Agency for Employment (*Bundesagentur für Arbeit*) as part of the Hartz reforms.
16. Until the end of 2004, Germany had three benefits relevant to unemployed: (1) contribution-based unemployment benefit (*Arbeitslosengeld*), defined as a percentage of former net income (60% or 67% without or with dependent children, respectively), no means-testing but of limited duration of normally 12 months. (2) Subsequent to the exhaustion of the eligibility period for (1), tax-funded unemployment assistance (*Arbeitslosenhilfe*) at replacement rates of 53% and 57% respectively, open-ended and means-tested. (3) Tax-funded social assistance (*Sozialhilfe*), flat rate, open-ended, means-tested, and available for all persons in need and unable to support themselves, irrespective of their employment status or history.
17. The new law states explicitly that the inferiority of the new job with respect to formal qualification or previously occupied positions cannot serve as a reason to reject the job. In addition, wages can be below local standards or collective agreements. The change of the sanction regime is the second push factor to activate jobseekers.
18. Germany does not know an all-encompassing minimum wage; only very few industries so far are regulated. Therefore, the low-wage sector – with wages down to US $3 per hour – has been growing extensively since the Hartz laws came into operation.
19. 'Niche occupation' refers to jobs like helping teachers to teach (the long-term unemployed are being called 'teacher aides'), gardeners to water plants or cut trees ('gardener aides'), or geriatric nurses to nurse old people ('nurse aides'), and so forth. Such job 'creation' is indeed 'entrepreneurial' and 'innovative.'
20. The reason for the PES' focus on persons instead of spaces is to be found in the different logics of local administrations and the still somewhat centralized PES – the latter being more concerned with 'target groups' within and accordingly out of the labor market and not with socio-economic developing strategies on the local scale (Eick et al., 2004).
21. The JobCenters have been created after the Hartz legislation for the management of long-term unemployed and further decentralized the PES structure.
22. 'Modellprojekt mit dem JobCenter startet im Januar' [Pilot scheme with JobCenter starts in January]. www.quartiersmanagement-berlin.de/3547.html (retrieved April 28, 2010).
23. Even though it would be misleading to compare safety and security measures in German schools with those, for example, in the USA (in Germany, fencing is not an issue, metal detectors are unknown, CCTV is of minor importance; but see W&S, 2008), security guards at school entrances nevertheless play a role; except for one district in Berlin, access control is not in the hands of rent-a-cops but in the hands of nonprofits (the same holds true for the re-emerging concept of the concierge in many multistory buildings); in the neighborhood management areas of the SIC program nonprofits do hold the monopoly (Eick, 2009).
24. A telling example here is the pride with which a representative of a Berlin nonprofit active in neighborhood management announced at a conference on 'Migration, Ghettos, and Parallel Societies': 'We have been able to arrange for the ending of a contract between the PES and a nonprofit active in streetwork, because we learned that the nonprofit refused to work together with the police – they don't get any monies any longer' (cited in Eick, 2008, pp. 93–94). Whereas police duties and those of public youth work are clearly separated – with respective legislation and differing logics of action – in the last years the blurring of such borders has intensified making it possible for strong stakeholders to argue for a *moral obligation* to cooperate with the police – even if the laws read differently.
25. Such a readjustment, for example, has been conducted by the Berlin JobCenter in the district of Charlottenburg-Wilmersdorf. The administration recognized that its labor

market (re)integration conceptions 'have been afflicted with the absence of means to prohibit the group of participants the opportunity of "escapism." The chance to get a job opportunity [i.e. one-Euro-job] has to be "guaranteed" no matter how long a "client" resists her "chance"' (JobCenter Charlottenburg-Wilmersdorf, 2009, p. 27, emphasis in original).

26. The term 'family' became popular in the recent past in areas as diverse as sports – 'the football family' (Forsyth, 2008) and 'the Olympic family'; international development – the World Bank (1998) talks about the 'social development family'; policing – 'the policing family' (Crawford & Lister, 2004) – and thus reflects the neocommunitarian paternalism of the different stakeholders even in their wording; the term 'neighborhood management family' has not yet emerged though.
27. www.bequit.de/aufsicht.htm (retrieved April 28, 2010).
28. All in all, 30 nonprofits provide security and order services for different customers (public and private) with different regional focal points.
29. www.jugendwohnen-berlin.de/concierge-maerkisches-viertel.0.html (retrieved April 28, 2010).
30. www.jugendwohnen-berlin.de/concierge-maerkisches-viertel.0.html (retrieved April 28, 2010).
31. With regard to the Roma families' apartments, the paper claims, 'the mere chance is to intensify on-site controls by the police and additional "leverages" such as the termination of rent-payments by the JobCenter, once the illegality of subletting rooms can be verified ... All projects need to be explained in all detail, alone to counteract the impression that in the future [the Task Force] heads for "to rule with an iron fist"' (Schmiedeknecht, 2009, pp. 10, 13). The strategic paper continues that, in order to control the drinkers, 'initially, officers of both the police and the municipal public order service should patrol the area on a weekly basis ... However, if the situation does not improve until 2009, the implementation of a bylaw prohibiting drinking should be considered' (Schmiedeknecht, 2009, pp. 17–18). Since January 2010, five long-term unemployed social workers are deployed as security guards – again, under the supervision of BEQUIT (Loy, 2010).
32. The districts are Kreuzberg, Friedrichshain, and Schöneberg, where 20 long-term unemployed are deployed to protect five schoolyards (Pham, 2007).
33. Since then, no more data are available, because, according to the administration, the collection of data 'is too voluminous and too expensive' (personal telephone conversation in August 2009); a current report, demanded by the political party Die Linke in January 2010, could only be analyzed elsewhere (Eick, 2009; Briken & Eick, 2011).
34. The city government of Münster, for example, with its roughly 270,000 residents and an unemployment rate of 5.9%, provides 130 long-term unemployed with one-Euro-jobs (July 2008), 80 of them do SOS services (Hanke, 2008, pp. 4–7). The city of Dresden, with its 510,000 residents and an unemployment rate of 11.6%, provides 3900 long-term unemployed with one-Euro-jobs (September 2009), 360 of them do SOS services. www.dresden.de/media/pdf/arge/Laufende_Massnahmen_ABM_ARGE_DD_Monat_April_2009.pdf (retrieved April 28, 2010).
35. A representative of the Senate of Berlin stated in an email to the author that 'I can try to collect the data' but – even after several further attempts – never supplied any data. A representative of Hamburg's Senate sent an email in June 2009, saying 'we no longer collect such data'; finally and also in June 2009, the research institute of the PES, the Institute for Employment and Research, claimed in an email to the author that 'an evaluation on your questions is not available' (personal communication).
36. Apart from that, the plethora of research reports that have been produced in order to better understand the financial, organizational, (re)integrative, and excluding effects of, in particular, the Hartz IV laws, is hardly comprehensible.
37. The financing arrangements in both labor market (re)integration and Hartz IV are just one example for why all stakeholders are willing to agree to an increased independence: the nation state together with the *Länder* provide the lion's share of monies (two-thirds in the SIC program) in order to meet their interest to devolve responsibilities while understanding their subsidies provided as an incentive for the stakeholders on the ground. The local state in turn should accept its responsibility to tackle the problems basically on its own; similar financial mechanisms apply to the PESs with its head office in Nuremberg, its regional dependences and the JobCenter.

References

Anderson, P. (2009). A new Germany? *New Left Review, 57*, 5–40.

Anheier, H.K., & Seibel, W. (1993). *Defining the nonprofit sector: Germany.* Baltimore, MD: The Johns Hopkins Institute for Policy Studies.

Baugesetzbuch. (2004). *2. Kapitel: Besonderes Städtebaurecht (§§ 136–191), 4. Teil – Soziale Stadt (§ 171e).* Berlin: Baugesetzbuch.

Becker, H., Thomas, F., Löhr, R.P., & Rösner, V. (2002). *Socially Integrative City program: An encouraging three-year appraisal.* Berlin: DIfU.

Berliner Kampagne gegen Hartz IV. (Ed.). (2008). *Wer nicht spurt, kriegt kein Geld. Sanktionen gegen Hartz-IV-Beziehende: Erfahrungen, Analysen, Schlussfolgerungen.* Berlin: Hartzkampagne.

BMVBS (Bundesministerium für Verkehr, Bau und Stadtentwicklung). (Ed.). (2008). *Status report: The program 'Social City': Summary.* Berlin: Bundesregierung.

BMVBS (Bundesministerium für Verkehr, Bau und Stadtentwicklung). (Ed.). (2009). *Jubiläumskongress 10 Jahre Soziale Stadt: Das Bund-Länder-Programm in der Praxis.* Berlin: Bundesregierung.

Bohne, E. (1981). *Der informelle Rechtsstaat: Eine empirische und rechtliche Untersuchung zum Gesetzesvollzug unter besonderer Berücksichtigung des Immissionsschutzes* [The Informal Constitutional State: An empirical and legal study on law enforcement in due consideration of immission control]. Berlin: Duncker & Humblot.

Boudreau, J.-A., Hamel, P., Jouve, B., & Keil, R. (2006). Comparing metropolitan governance: The cases of Montreal and Toronto. *Progress in Planning, 66*(1), 7–59.

Brenner, N. (2001). The limits to scale? Methodological reflections on scalar structuration. *Progress in Human Geography, 25*(4), 591–614.

Brenner, N., Jessop, B., Jones, M., & MacLeod, G. (Eds.). (2003). *State/space: A reader.* Oxford: Blackwell.

Brenner, N., & Theodore, N. (2002). Cities and the geographies of 'Actually Existing Neoliberalism.' In N. Brenner & N. Theodore (Eds.), *Spaces of neoliberalism* (pp. 2–32). Oxford: Blackwell.

Briken, K., & Eick, V. (2011). Recht und billig? Wachschutz zwischen Niedriglohn und Ein-Euro-Jobs [Right and proper? Rent-a-cops between low wages and one-Euro-jobs]. *Kritische Justiz, 44*(1), in print.

Bundesregierung. (Ed.). (2009). *Unterrichtung durch die Bundesregierung: Stadtentwicklungsbericht 2008* (printed matter 16/13130, May 6). Berlin: Deutscher Bundestag.

Bundestransferstelle Soziale Stadt. (Ed.). (2008). *Statusbericht 2008 zum Programm Soziale Stadt.* Berlin: BMVB.

Crawford, A., & Lister, S. (2004). *The extended policing family. Visible patrols in residential areas.* Leeds: Joseph Rowntree Foundation.

Deggerich, M. (2007). Jugendliche: Drei Engel für Kreuzberg [Adolescents: Three angels for Kreuzberg]. *Der Spiegel, 38*(September 17), 58.

Dingeldey, I. (2009). *Activating labor market policies and the restructuring of 'welfare' and 'state.'* Bremen: Zentrum für Sozialpolitik.

Dubber, M.D., & Valverde, M. (Eds.). (2008). *Police and the liberal state.* Stanford, CA: Stanford University Press.

Dworkin, A. (1981). *Pornography: Men possessing women.* New York: Perigee Books.

Ehrke, M. (1999). *Revisionism revisited: The Third Way and European social democracy.* Retrieved April 21, 2010, from http://library.fes.de/pdf-files/bueros/suedafrika/02824.pdf

Eichhorst, W., Grienberger-Zingerle, M., & Konle-Seidl, R. (2006). *Activation policies in Germany: From status protection to basic income support.* Bonn: IZA.

Eick, V. (2003). New strategies of policing the poor. *Policing & Society, 4*(13), 365–379.

Eick, V. (2007). Space patrols. The new peace-keeping functions of nonprofits. In H. Leitner, J. Peck, & E. Sheppard (Eds.), *Contesting neoliberalism: The urban frontier* (pp. 266–290). New York: Guilford Press.

Eick, V. (2008). Urbane Wachen und die neuen Polizeien [Urban guards and the new policing forces]. In F. Arndt, C. Dege, C. Ellermann, M. Mayer, D. Teller, & L. Zimmermann (Eds.), *Ordnungen im Wandel* (pp. 81–104). Bielefeld: transcript.

Eick, V. (2009). Hartz IV kommt jetzt in 'Uniform' [Hartz IV now strolls around in 'uniforms']. In A. Allex & D. Kalkan (Eds.), *Ausgesteuert: ausgegrenzt ... angeblich asozial* (pp. 301–311). Neu-Ulm: AG SPAK.

Eick, V., Mayer, M., Grell, B., & Sambale, J. (2004). *Nonprofit-Organisationen und die Transformation der lokalen Beschäftigungspolitik* [Nonprofit organizations and the transformation of the local employment policy]. Münster: Westfälisches Dampfboot.

Eisenschitz, A., & Gough, J. (1996). The contradictions of neo-Keynesian local economic strategy. *Review of International Political Economy, 3*(3), 434–458.

England, K., & Ward, K. (Eds.). (2007). *Neoliberalization: States, networks, peoples.* Oxford: Blackwell.

Etzioni, A. (1996). *The new golden rule: Community and morality in a democratic society.* New York: Basic Books.

Evers, A. (1995). Part of the welfare mix: The Third Sector as an intermediate area. *Voluntas, 6*(2), 159–182.

Forsyth, R. (2008, February 8). FIFA and UEFA's 'Football family' horror show. *telegraph.co.uk.* Retrieved April 21, 2010, from http://www.telegraph.co.uk/sport/football/2291239/Fifa-and-Uefas-Football-family-horror-show.html

Frank, S. (2005). Eine kurze Geschichte der 'europäischen Stadtpolitik': erzählt in drei Sequenzen [A short story about 'European city politics': Narrated in three sequences]. *Planungsrundschau, 11*, 307–324.

Freie und Hansestadt Hamburg. (Ed.). (2006). *Umsetzung und Ergebnisse der öffentlich geförderten Arbeitsgelegenheiten nach § 16 (3) SGB II im Jahr 2005.* Hamburg: Behörde für Wirtschaft und Arbeit.

Fritsche, M. (2003). *Neues Regieren im Quartier? Das Beispiel Kottbusser Tor in Berlin-Kreuzberg* [New governance in the quarter? The example of Kottbusser Tor in the district of Berlin-Kreuzberg]. Berlin: Freie Universität Berlin.

Fuchs, C. (2005, August 1). Als Dienstkleidung ein weißes Shirt mit Sonne [T-shirts with a sun-emblem as working clothes]. *Berliner Zeitung*, 9.

Fyfe, N.R. (2005). Making space for 'neo-communitarianism'? The Third Sector, state and civil society in the UK. *Antipode, 37*(3), 536–557.

Gern, W., & Segbers, F. (Eds.). (2009). *Als Kunde bezeichnet, als Bettler behandelt: Erfahrungen aus der Hartz IV-Welt* [Referred to as a customer, treated as a beggar: Experiences from the Hartz IV world]. Hamburg: VSA.

Giddens, A. (1998). *The Third Way: The renewal of social democracy.* Cambridge: Polity Press.

Goodin, R.E. (2003). Democratic accountability: The distinctiveness of the Third Sector. *European Journal of Sociology, 44*(3), 359–396.

Hanke, A. (2008). *Umsetzung des § 16 Absatz 3 SGB II bei der Stadt Münster: Arbeitsgelegenheiten mit Mehraufwandsentschädigung.* Münster: ms.

Hans Böckler Stiftung. (Ed.). (2006). *Die 'Hartz-Reform' und ihre Folgen.* Düsseldorf: Hans Böckler Stiftung.

Harvey, D. (1989). From managerialism to entrepreneurialism: The transformation in urban governance in late capitalism. *Geografiska Annaler, 71B*(1), 3–17.

Häußermann, H. (2005). Das Programm 'Stadtteile mit besonderem Entwicklungsbedarf – die Soziale Stadt' [The program 'Neighborhoods with a particular need for renewal – The socially integrative city']. *Informationen zur Raumentwicklung, 2*(3), 75–85.

Häußermann, H., & Kapphan, A. (2000). *Berlin: Von der geteilten zur gespaltenen Stadt? Sozialräumlicher Wandel seit 1990* [Berlin: From the divided to the polarized city? Sociospatial change since 1990]. Opladen: Leske + Budrich.

Helms, G. (2008). *Towards safe city centres? Remaking the spaces of an old-industrial city.* Aldershot: Ashgate.

Henry, A., & Smith, D.J. (Eds.). (2007). *Transformations of policing.* Aldershot: Ashgate.

Holm, A. (2001). Behutsame Verdrängung am Helmholtzplatz: Ausgrenzung im Aufwerungsgebiet [Scrupulous displacement at the Helmholtz square. Exclusion within a value-added quarter]. *MieterEcho, 286*, 8–9.

Hömberg, U. (2007). Wie steht es um die Sauberkeit? [How is it going with cleanliness?] *Promenadenpost, 4*(7), 7.

IfS (Institut für Stadtforschung und Strukturpolitik GmbH). (Ed.). (2004). *Die soziale Stadt.* Berlin: Bundesamt für Bauwesen und Raumordnung.

Ilcan, S., & Basok, T. (2004). Community government: Voluntary agencies, social justice, and the responsibilization of citizens. *Citizenship Studies, 8*(2), 129–144.

Jacobs, S. (2008, December 2). Schulen im Problembezirk: Die Torschützer von Neukölln [Schools within the problem quarter. The gatekeepers of Neukölln]. *Der Tagesspiegel*, 9.

Jessop, B. (2002). Liberalism, neoliberalism, and urban governance: A state-theoretical perspective. In N. Brenner & N. Theodore (Eds.), *Spaces of neoliberalism* (pp. 105–125). Oxford: Blackwell.

Jessop, B., Brenner, N., & Jones, M. (2008). Theorizing sociospatial relations. *Environment and Planning D: Society and Space, 26*(3), 389–401.

JobCenter Charlottenburg-Wilmersdorf. (Ed.). (2009). *Arbeitsmarktprogramm 2009: Verbesserung der Integration in Erwerbstätigkeit und Vermeidung von Langzeitbezug* [Employment program 2009: Improvement of labor market integration and avoidance of long-term unemployment]. Berlin: ms.

Jones, T., & Newburn, T. (Eds.). (2007). *Plural policing: A comparative perspective.* New York: Routledge.

Klute, J. (2008). Die Zukunft der Arbeit und ihre Destruktion durch die Hartz-Reformen [The future of work and its destruction by the Hartz legislation]. In J. Klute & S. Kotlenga (Eds.), *Sozial- und Arbeitsmarktpolitik nach Hartz. Fünf Jahre Hartzreformen* (pp. 169–177). Göttingen: Universitätsverlag Göttingen.

Knuth, M. (2009). Path shifting and path dependence: Labor market policy reforms under German federalism. *International Journal of Public Administration, 32*(12), 1048–1069.

Kotlenga, S. (2008). Auswirkungen der Hartz-Reformen auf den Dritten Sektor [Ramifications of the Hartz reforms on the Third Sector]. In J. Klute & S. Kotlenga (Eds.), *Sozial- und Arbeitsmarktpolitik nach Hartz. Fünf Jahre Hartzreformen* (pp. 100–121). Göttingen: Universitätsverlag Göttingen.

Krummacher, M., Kulbach, R., Waltz, V., & Wohlfahrt, N. (2003). *Soziale Stadt, Sozialraumentwicklung, Quartiersmanagement* [Social city, networking in the local community, neighborhood management]. Opladen: Leske + Budrich.

Lake, R.W., & Newman, K. (2002). Differential citizenship in the shadow state. *GeoJournal, 58*(2–3), 109–120.

Lanz, S. (2000). Der Staat verordnet die Zivilgesellschaft [The state prescribes the civil society]. *Widersprüche, 78*(20), 39–52.

Lauff, G. (2010). Global denken, lokal handeln – der Mehrwert integrierter Förderstrategien auf lokaler Ebene [Think globally, act locally – The added value of integrated support strategies for the local level]. *PUNKT. Das Magazin aus Berlin über die Europäischen Strukturfonds, 19*(97), 6–8.

Lauria, M. (Ed.). (1997). *Reconstructing urban regime theory: Regulating urban politics in a global economy.* Thousand Oaks, CA: Sage.

Lavelle, A.D. (2007). Social democracy or neo-liberalism? The cases of Sweden and Germany. In G. Curran & E.V. Acker (Eds.), *Globalising government business relations* (pp. 117–144). Frenchs Forest: Pearson.

Lawless, P. (2006). Area-based urban interventions: Rationale and outcomes – The new deal for communities programme in England. *Urban Studies, 43*(11), 1991–2011.

Leber, S. (2005, June 2). Im Einsatz auf den Spielplätzen: Ein-Euro-Jobber sollen dazu beitragen, dass Kinder ungestört toben können [In the line of duty on the playgrounds: One-Euro-jobbers are to contribute to children's ability to frolic]. *Der Tagesspiegel*, 9.

Leitner, H., Peck, J., & Sheppard, E. (Eds.). (2007). *Contesting neoliberalism: Urban frontiers.* New York: Guilford Press.

Logan, J.R., & Molotch, H.L. (1987). *Urban fortunes: The political economy of place.* Berkeley: University of California Press.

Loy, T. (2010, March 10). Schillerkiez: Eingreiftruppe für das Problemviertel [Boardwalk Schillerkiez: Rapid response team for the problem quarter]. *Der Tagesspiegel*, 7.

Márquez, F.B., & Pérez, F.P. (2008). Spatial frontiers and neo-communitarian identities in the city: The case of Santiago de Chile. *Urban Studies, 45*(7), 1461–1483.

Martens, K. (2002). Mission impossible? Defining nongovernmental organizations. *Voluntas, 13*(3), 271–285.

Mayer, M. (1994). Post-Fordist city politics. In A. Amin (Ed.), *Post-Fordism: A reader* (pp. 316–337). Oxford: Basil Blackwell.

Mayer, M. (2007). Contesting the neoliberalization of urban governance. In H. Leitner, J. Peck, & E. Sheppard (Eds.), *Contesting neoliberalism: Urban frontiers* (pp. 90–115). New York: Guilford Press.

Mayer, M. (2009). Combating social exclusion with 'activating' policies. *The Urban Reinventors*. Retrieved April 21, 2010, from http://www.urbanreinventors.net/3/mayer/mayer-urbanreinventors.pdf

McCarthy, J. (2005). Devolution in the woods: Community forestry as hybrid neoliberalism. *Environment and Planning A, 37*(6), 995–1014.

Morris, S. (2000). Defining the nonprofit sector: Some lessons from history. *Voluntas, 11*(1), 25–43.

Müller, E. (2009). *Die Armutsindustrie* [The poverty industry]. Retrieved December 20, 2010, from http://www.youtube.com/watch?v=iDIeWhTCItI

Novy, A., & Hammer, E. (2007). Radical innovation in the era of liberal governance: The case of Vienna. *European Urban and Regional Studies, 14*(3), 210–222.

Osborne, D., & Gaebler, T. (1992). *Reinventing government*. Reading, MA: Addison-Wesley.

Peck, J. (2001). *Workfare states*. London: Guilford Press.

Peck, J., & Tickell, A. (2002). Neoliberalizing space. *Antipode, 34*(3), 380–404.

Pham, K. (2007). *Gewalt an Schulen. Als Ein-Euro-Schutzmann auf dem Pausenh of.* Retrieved April 21, 2010, from http://www.spiegel.de/schulspiegel/0,1518,464981,00.html

Rose, N. (1996). The death of the social? Re-figuring the territory of government. *Economy and Society, 25*(3), 327–356.

Salamon, L.M. (Ed.). (2002). *The state of nonprofit America*. Washington, DC: Brookings Institution Press.

Schmid, R. (2006, January). 'Big Steps' und Conciergedienste: Sozialer Service für das Wohngebiet [Concierge service 'Big Steps': Providing social services for the residential area]. *Nachrichten Parität. Für Berlin*, 6–9.

Schmiedeknecht, K. (2009). *TFO – Task Force Okerstraße: Strategiekonzept*. Retrieved April 21, 2010, from http://media.de.indymedia.org/media/2009/07//255733.pdf

Schmiemann, B. (2010, February 2). Jobcenter Neukölln bezieht Büroturm im Kindl-Boulevard [JobCenter Neukölln moves into office highrise at Kindle boulevard]. *Berliner Morgenpost*, 11.

Schulze-Böing, M. (2000). Leitbild 'aktivierende Stadt.' Konzepte zur aktivierenden Sozialpolitik und Arbeitsförderung auf kommunaler Ebene [Model 'activating city.' Concepts for activating social policy and employment promotion on the municipal level]. In E. Mezger & K.W. West (Eds.), *Aktivierender Sozialstaat und politisches Handeln* (pp. 51–62). Marburg: Schüren.

Schuster, S. (2003). Utrechter Platz: Aufwerten durch Abräumen [Utrecht square: Gentrifying by making a clean sweep]. *Berliner MieterMagazin, 6*, 12–13.

Scraton, P. (2004). Streets of terror: Marginalization, criminalization and authoritarian renewal. *Social Justice, 31*(1–2), 130–158.

Senat von Berlin. (Ed.). (2008). *Rahmenstrategie Soziale Stadtentwicklung – auf dem Weg zu einer integrierten Stadt(teil)entwicklung in Berlin*. Berlin: Projektgruppe Rahmenstrategie.

Smith, A., Stenning, A., & Willis, K. (Eds.). (2008). *Social justice and neoliberalism: Global perspectives*. New York: Zed Books.

Smith, D.M. (1998). How far should we care? On the spatial scope of beneficence. *Progress in Human Geography, 22*(1), 15–38.

Spitzer, S. (1975). Toward a Marxian theory of deviance. *Social Problems, 22*(5), 638–651.

Swyngedouw, E. (1997). Neither global nor local: 'Glocalisation' and the politics of scale. In K. Cox (Ed.), *Spaces of globalization* (pp. 137–166). New York: Guilford Press.

Tam, H. (1998). *Communitarianism. A new agenda for politics and citizenship*. New York: Palgrave.

Tok, E. (2009). *Varieties of neoliberal communitarianism in the cities of Anatolia-Turkey*. Paper presented at the conference of the Canadian Political Science Association 2009. Retrieved April 21, 2010, from http://www.cpsa-acsp.ca/papers-2009/Tok.pdf

ver.di (Vereinte Dienstleistungsgewerkschaft) Berlin-Brandenburg. (Ed.). (2007). *Ein-Euro-Jobs, Zusatzjobs, MAE ... Synonym für eine gescheiterte Reform* [One-Euro-jobs, allowances, additional work ... Synonym for a failed reform]. Berlin: ver.di.

Vogelsang, L. (2010, March 8). Ein Gefühl von Sicherheit [A feeling of security]. *Der Tagesspiegel*, 9.

W&S. Das Sicherheitsmagazin. (2008). Abschreckende Kamera. Schulzentrum Tarp setzt Videoüberwachung gegen Vandalismus ein [Deterrent cameras: School center in the village of Tarp deploys video surveillance against vandalism]. *W&S. Wirtschaft & Sicherheit, 12*, 28.

Wallace, A. (2007). 'We have had nothing for so long that we don't know what to ask for': New deal for communities and the regeneration of socially excluded terrain. *Social Policy and Society, 6*(1), 1–12.

Wood, J., & Dupont, B. (Eds.). (2006). *Democracy, society and the governance of security*. Cambridge: Cambridge University Press.

World Bank. (Ed.). (1998). *The initiative on defining, monitoring and measuring social capital: Overview and program description*. Washington, DC: The World Bank.

The space between the steps: reckoning in an era of reconciliation

Michelle Stewart[1]

Department of Anthropology, University of California Davis, Davis, CA 95616, USA

For over 100 years the government of Canada operated residential schools for Aboriginal children that required children be taken out of their homes and educated away from their families. These schools became sites of widespread abuse, the legacy of which continues to influence the lives of those who attended and the generations that followed. As Canada moves through a reconciliation process that includes reparation payments, official apologies, and Truth Commissions, this article considers other modalities that happen in the space between the expected flow from apology to reconciliation and resolution. Based on ethnographic fieldwork with the Royal Canadian Mounted Police, this article considers the ways in which a community crime prevention workshop is transformed into a different type of *work* space as participants engage in problem solving by discussing the role of residential schools in daily life. They do so in meetings with police officers who represent one of the branches of government associated to the enforcement of this colonial policy. By considering these situated practices, this chapter will consider alternate modalities that must reckon with the legacy of residential schools.

> Canada built an educational system in which very young children were forcibly removed from their homes, often taken far from their communities ... The government now recognizes that the consequences of the Indian residential schools policy were profoundly negative and that this policy has had a lasting and damaging impact on Aboriginal culture, heritage and language.[2]

This article considers a police-sponsored, community crime prevention workshop that took place in a remote village during a time in which the Canadian state was attempting to recognize the effects of its colonial past. The workshop, created and sponsored by the Royal Canadian Mounted Police (RCMP),[3] is a full two-day event[4] that is often hosted in predominantly Aboriginal communities. Falling within the larger practices of community policing[5] (Brunschot, 2003; Cattelino, 2004; Chesluk, 2004; Das & Lab, 2003; Gianakis & Davis, 1998; Reed, 1999; Tilley, 2005), the workshop was developed as way to facilitate collaboration with community members. In effect it acts as a training event that seeks to condition police and the public to work together on crime prevention programs. One of the goals of which is the offloading of certain types of police work which involves asking members of the public to take 'responsibility' (and be accountable) for more minor policing needs. This reordering allows police to engage in more 'targeted' (efficient) policing (Bullock, Erol, & Tilley, 2006; Burnett, 2007; Everson, 2003; Mawby & Worrall, 2004).

Created for smaller towns, but hosted predominantly in Aboriginal communities, the workshop takes on a new life when it exits RCMP regional offices and arrives in a local Aboriginal community. Due in part to the historical relationship between Aboriginal peoples and police, and the current political moment focused on reconciliation, the workshop is transformed. Based on 15 months of ethnographic research with the RCMP, this article considers how these workshops about crime prevention and collaboration (from a policing perspective) can yield a different experience when participants must engage in the *work* of reckoning. By looking at the situated practices (Haraway, 1988) of one workshop to explore the layered context in which it is delivered reveals the challenge of macro-scale reconciliation and locates unexpected micro-scale negotiations at play in these workshops. Held during the era of national reconciliation replete with Truth and Reconciliation Commissions, Reparation Payments, National and Church Apologies, this article contextualizes the workshops to better understand the sort of *work* that takes place in these settings and investigate alternate modalities that operate at the limits of reconciliation. Formal apologies and reconciliation can attempt to produce a certain type of movement, steps, towards 'closure.' This article seeks to disrupt some of the presumptions that surround that movement and speak instead about the spaces between the steps.

Anthropologist Diane Nelson, when speaking of the aftermath of the civil war in Guatemala, takes up the idea of reckoning and states: 'Reckoning can mean to count, to figure up; to measure possibilities for the future; and to settle rewards or penalties for action. It promises clarity, an accounting or balancing out' (Nelson, 2009, p. xiv). Here she speaks of the accounting logic within reckoning; to reckon is to balance out, to even the scorecard. For some, reconciliation might be a form of reckoning in which the state attempts to balance out the effect of its own misdeeds (through payments, apologies, tribunals, etc). I want to switch the lens and ask under what conditions are things *reckoned with*. By reckon with, I mean the ways in which individuals must wrestle with those things left unaccounted. This form of reckoning, that does not specifically seek to balance out, can be a space of productive tension. The article will discuss a crime prevention workshop that, when situated in practice, became a space of reckoning as participants had to wrestle with the legacy of residential schools as part of their work.

For police, the goal of the workshop series is to bring police and community together to discussed and prioritized community problems so that 'the community can take responsibility for its own issues' as one officer explained. Indeed, this mode of policing is asking officers to take a step back from their community involvement and to reconsider the terms of police work. A senior officer often articulated to me that police have become over-invested in communities, commonly identifiable by police being central participants in various youth and after-school programs, and that this type of policing had to come to an end. 'We can no longer be everything to everyone,' he would assert because this type of policing is 'unsustainable.' This is a language of efficiency and accountability. By rejecting the paternalist role, police managers articulate a new era in the business of policing that focused on targeted, intelligence-led policing. The transition into this new modality of policing required that police *compel* community members to take responsibility for certain problems that could be assigned to working groups. This assignment of responsibility and rejection of paternalistic police practice is indicative of neoliberal practices that pin responsibility to communities deemed *capable* of solving their own problems.[6] Seen this way the framework is that police recognize the ability of the residents to resolve their own problems and that residents are expected to articulate to the police, within this workshop mode, a set of discrete 'solvable' problems. However, situated in practice the workshop reveals a different framework for understanding the problems that needed to be reckoned with. Specifically, the workshop offers a glimpse into the ways in which community members understand and articulate local problems in a distinct relationship with residential schools. In an era of official apologies and national programs for reconciliation the workshop becomes an unexpected place in which other conversations can take place about this part of Canada's history and its continued effect on the lives of people and communities.

Just visiting – situating police services

It is a crisp morning on the small northern island (Figure 1). It is the first day of a pilot workshop on crime prevention. It is the third such workshop I have attended in the past month; the routine is understood as we stack into the police trucks and head down to the community center. We drive slowly as the road kicks up a powdery-winter mix that dusts the cars and shrubs. Causal and at times awkward waves are exchanged between local Aboriginal residents and the visiting police officers. Sitting in the back of the police car, without a uniform, I get a curious look and reserved wave. Weaving through the village we pass the Methodist Church, red paint weathered by salt air, its steeple presses into the sky. We make another turn and arrive at the community center.

Figure 1. View of the village from the boardwalk (all photos are taken by author).

'Here we go,' one of the officer nods his head as he exits, I knock on the window to remind him to unlock and release me from the custody of the back seat. Walking up to the center a group of children slow their play to pay us some attention I can see we are being sized up. 'Are you RCMP?' one child asks me. I smile and shake my head 'no.'

In this small community the RCMP has a relatively small role in daily life. Unlike many communities that have an RCMP detachment[7] (or many) and officers with regular shifts in which they respond to calls, investigate crimes, and patrol neighborhoods this small island sits outside many of the understandings one might have about policing. In this community police come when they are called for service and maintain a relatively limited active presence. Officers tell me that they patrol when they can but with limited resources the patrols become sparse at times. I am asked frequently if I am an RCMP officer on this trip. Later I will be told that residents have come to expect new faces (new officers) each time the police come to the island.

Police services are coordinated at a small police substation located at the mainland harbor. Officers are associated to the larger regional police station but coordinate the daily work of policing these remote communities from the small station and from their boats. Nestled in a series of coastal villages, the island community is an hour-long boat ride followed by a one-hour car ride on washer-board, switchback roads. Because of this isolation officers report that the most common police services these villages receive are those delivered under duress or in the event of a death. An emergency call in these communities requires the preparation of boats and coordination of logistics on both sides, 'at the shortest, it is a couple hours to get there if there is an emergency.' Some communities are so distant officers pop a raspberry if you ask how long an emergency response would take. One officer tells me that they visit the community frequently, but another concedes, 'We come as often as we can but it is logistically quite difficult – we don't get up here as often as we'd like.' Adding that this community is the 'quietest' of the three they patrol, it receives the least amount of police attention. In these remote settings, the RCMP goal is to provide a police presence a few days a month, in each of the coastal communities. A couple of days of police presence is meant to provide the time needed for residents to convey concerns and for officers to perform other functions such as DARE programming. In practicality, the police *visit* the communities and when they do, locals joke: each time a police truck drives up, a different, younger, officer gets out. It is the butt of some jokes but acts to set one of the relational frameworks of policing: the police as visitor.

'We are a transient organization,' is a common phrase used by RCMP officers. Transient here serves to underscore the ways in which police move in and out of communities. This movement is only amplified when visiting smaller communities, rural policing locations. This type of policing is a special appointment for officers – and often one of their first after police training. Because it is remote and isolated, officers are only permitted to work in the area for a short period of time before they are transferred to work in a different community.

On the island, the RCMP–community relationship is a product of infrequent visits, and reflects the transient state of relations that have only been exacerbated by other bureaucratic influences. On the drive into the community, officers explained that they did not currently have a detachment but instead that they rented a house because the federal and provincial governments are not allowed to own land or structures on Aboriginal lands and/or on reserve. This bureaucratic constraint has resulted in a juggernaut with regards to *where* the police are located on the island.

A few years ago, the police detachment was declared an unsafe workspace because of the invasion of dangerous molds that was causing many officers to get sick when on patrol. The RCMP and tribal council were in negotiations about the cost-share on building a new police station. But with negotiations stalled for some time, the RCMP now rents a two-storey house at the end of the village that serves as sleeping quarters when officers come to town. Over time the officers have fashioned a holding area out of the downstairs' basement. Most of the time the house sits empty. But when the police are in town they live in the house that sits in the middle of the main neighborhood – the last house on the street. Police presence on the island and as occasional neighbor is a strange affair. Residents often announce on two-way radio when police are in town based on sightings in the village or the presence of the car at the house. Rather than call the police (on the mainland) who will then dispatch the officers (from another location in the province), residents simply walk up to the house and knock on the door or call the house directly at times to seek assistance or 'just talk' with the officers. As we drive around, one officer describes the local issues facing the fisheries and tells stories of children as they pass by. For some officers there is an intimacy, a familiarity. In many ways this what it means to police in rural settings; intimate as people walk up for a chat at the house, but also distant because departure is imminent.

Reckoning with the past and contextualizing local 'problems'

The first thing to greet participants as they walk into the workshop is the table of flyers and business cards for different agencies and projects. The previous day the RCMP officer involved in coordinating the meeting explained many different counselors would be in attendance, he nodded his head 'just in case something comes up in the workshop.' Not entirely sure what specifically could come up at the workshop I did not press him at the time. A quick scan of the table the next day revealed a wealth of resources that ranged from support services for survivors of sexual assault and historic sexual assault alongside suicide prevention, alcohol and drug counseling as well as traditional healing services. I had watched the workshop get revised with attention to many issues facing Aboriginal peoples. However, in attending meetings, I had not seen this same presence of resources and services made so visible.

These workshops were designed by planners at regional police headquarters and operate, in some ways, as a diagnostic tool such that crime becomes preventable if the community can cure what ails it (drug use, alcoholism, vandalism, violence, etc.). Standardized teaching modules are written in such a way that 'problem solving' between police and community is given value because it comes with the understanding that problems outlined in the workshop can then be taken up by community members and not be seen as police work. The goal is to have members of the community attend the workshop and help to co-produce a list of 'problems' facing the community, then police alongside community members and individuals from local social service agencies prioritize the list, vote, and elect the top four or five issues in the community and then come up with a plan to correct the issue. This process of selecting the top issues facing the community is predicated on the principles of liberal democracy[8] with the end result understood to be the practice of collaboration. However, in this setting, a collaboration of this type appeared to require a battalion of support services able to absorb the potential revelations and impact of these conversations between police and residents on local problems.

Figure 2. The workshop space is organized around the idea of group work. Tables are arranged with a limited number of work books, upon entering the workshop each participant must chose a seat and a group to work with.

As people filed into the meeting room a mix of new and old faces produced the quiet chatter of introductions. A local woman, who agreed to be the co-facilitator for the workshop, smiled and greeted participants as they walked in. One of the police officers leaned over and pointed out the prominent community members to us as they took their seats. Quiet calculations were taking place in the crowd as notice was given of who did and did not choose to attend this event.

The meeting quickly became a mix of local residents, police officers, and regional agency workers (nurses that visit occasionally, youth outreach workers from the mainland, crisis support workers from the island and mainland, other mental health workers and police from the mainland). As participants filtered in and took seats, many elders chose to sit on the sofa and chairs that lined the walls rather than the large tables set up for participants. Though urged by the visiting RCMP facilitator and representative to sit at the tables, most smiled politely and looked away, satisfied with their seat selection. And while some sat quietly on the couch, some of the other elders were a bit more lively, heckling their children and grandchildren, nieces and nephews as they entered the room.

The workshop was being hosted in the Elders Lodge – a large meeting room attached to the larger community center. Transformed from a general meeting room into a workshop space required that tables be reoriented to face a projector screen and each table to be set up with a set or resources including a binder for each participant, a set of pens and markers, name tags, and post-it notes (for an example, see Figure 2). An hour before the meeting we transformed the room into that space. Trying to use all the seats available we were limited to seven chairs per table and eight large tables that could comfortably fit facing the same direction. As people walked in they slowly situated themselves at tables after appraising the room and potential table-mates. I stood in the corner waiting to see if there would be adequate space to join a table.

'Oh, are they joining us this morning?' a woman asked me as youth from the local school walked in with their teacher and principal. She seemed pleasantly surprised, I responded, 'I think they are going to be here for the whole thing?' looking to the facilitator to confirm my answer, he nodded and I watched many eyes follow the group as the teacher organized the students around two tables. The students attempted to quiet as they sat around tables, under the noticeable eye of parents, aunties, uncles, and grandparents. Noticing one spot open I took my seat with the students before we started.

Bob,[9] the visiting RCMP facilitator loudly welcomed the group and officially started the workshop by introducing his local co-facilitator Janice, the local woman who had been greeting people as they entered. Bob offered Janice as a great community 'asset' expressing his gratitude in working with her and informed the group she would be the point person for future meetings and follow up after the workshop. A bit uncomfortable with all eyes on her, she shrugged off the responsibility, 'I don't really know how I got here,' she joked. Bob chuckled, not an orchestrated banter, it read awkward as Bob feigned familiarity. Smiling, he turned back to the audience and slapped his hands together. 'OK, well let's go ahead and get things started,' rubbing his hands together, as one might do before they create a wondrous thing, his eyebrows popped up, and he nodded his head in the direction of the back of the room. He told the group they would start with a set of introductions and asked participants 'why you are here and what you hope to gain from this workshop?' I was a bit surprised by the invitation. The previous day, during a police planning session, discussion included the need to limit introductions to ensure the workshop stayed on schedule. Whether purposeful or not, Bob's question to the crowd served to dismiss the scheduling concern. One-by-one, participants took control of the schedule as introductions became the first order of business.

'Well most of you know me, but since we do have visitors,' many residents began as they acknowledged the outsiders attending the meeting. These introductions served to illustrate to both local residents and visitors the many strengths of the community by vocalizing the coming together of the elders, council members, other community leaders and residents to affirm relationships and commitments. These introductions also served to remind visitors (specifically non-Aboriginal visitors) whose land they were standing on. Introductions served to politely remind visitors who was in charge of the meeting; visitors were, at best, invited to assist. 'I would like to thank the counselors who have come to help.' Some of the non-local residents were members of other regional tribes and would identify their tribal association during their introduction while expressing gratitude for being invited to participate as a visitor. From political affiliations to kinship ties, the introductions though informal, were formal in asserting relations and the terms of participation.

'There are a lot aunties and uncles in this room,' a council member introduced himself and thanked everyone in attendance. As his eyes swept across the room he spoke about the traditional role of aunties and uncles in the community as disciplinarians such that children were 'kept in line' without being upset with their parents. He looked directly at the youth in attendance and told them of the importance of their participation in the workshop and the need to respect the privilege. 'I see my nephew over there,' his eyes met the stare of a young man. Without aggression, only strong assertion, he told the students to pay attention because they are the future of the community and they must listen to their aunties and uncles in this room. As he took his seat, some shifted in their seats as a silent communication of aunties and uncles to nieces and nephews appeared through nods and smiles. Sitting with most of the youth, and their anglo-instructor, I noticed this exchange of looks and found it interesting that his instructions did not tell them to listen to their teacher or to the facilitator. Rather than lip service to niceties, his instructions focused on the brass tacks of obedience:

look around the room, find your auntie and/or uncle, that is your anchor and that is who you are answerable to in this room.

'Everything we did to fight the government, everything we do today, we do for you so you don't have to go through the same thing we did,' another man reminded the students of the shared history of the group. A history of colonialism that is, itself, entwined in the history of the RCMP – the police charged with enforcing colonial rules upon Aboriginal peoples. His eye is trained on one young man in particular. In this small community everyone is related by a few degrees to each other. He breaks his stare as a woman introduces herself. He returns to his coffee as she begins to speak on the importance of youth inclusion, 'It is important to invite the kids so they can learn. But usually they are only allowed to stay for an hour … and you can't learn anything in an hour' she expresses support for their attendance and the need to grant them the rights to full participation. She speaks as the auntie who will reprimand and the advocate who will fight for their rights. A month later, I attended another workshop in a different community in which groups of students are shuffled in for a two-hour rotation during the workshop. For these participants, notepads were used for doodles and note passing because the role of youth participation was entirely unclear. In this workshop, students were not asked to be participants but rather to simply watch what was happening. Whereas a workshop with full youth participation, in which youth introduced themselves, did all the exercises, and were listened to, would mean they were given status as full participants.

Alongside recognition of youth participation, there was gratitude for elders. One man stands up and many in the crowd smile affectionately – from this vantage point he appears to hold a strong place in the community. After introducing himself as the local language instructor he concedes, 'less than 15 of us know how to speak the language.' He shakes his head and discusses the language classes he holds at the school – but, he explains, the language is fading quickly. Looking to the corners of the room, he speaks to the elders clustered together on sofas. He speaks to them for a few minutes, not in English, most in the crowd do not understand the exchange but watch and listen. Elders nod with him in agreement. He tells the group that in the past they would hold community language classes but people stopped attending, now he can only teach the children and as he tries to find others who can speak with him. He expresses excitement about the youth involvement and then launches into an animated conversation about the documentary crew that visited the island for their project focused on native languages. He tells the group that the video will soon begin traveling around the world. As he sits down, an elder gets up stating simply, 'We used to be invited to talk in the school and I hope that door will be open again.' He turns to school principal, herself a local Aboriginal (unlike many of the teachers[10]). She nods and looks away as he takes his seat. In these introductions it becomes clear that despite the large turn-out and relative cohesion of the community, there is a large set of challenges facing the group. In this opening, some 'problems' are eluded to but not discussed openly in this mixed crowd of residents and visitors, of Aboriginal and non-Aboriginal, of those who understand and those who are learning.

A participant stands up and introduces herself; she says that she wants to talk about 'the fire' and offers comments directed both to the residents and the visitors, 'It happens in the white community, it happens in Japan – we are getting good advice from our elders about the bad times we have had here.' Seemingly fragmented thoughts receive unanimous nods; the gaps in the sentence are filled in throughout the introductions as it becomes clear that there has been a series of fires and vandalism that have had strong affects on the community. The relief came through good advice that would allow community members to tackle the issue. For some it was important to talk to the elders and seek their guidance to stop these activities. The elders, in these conversations, are understood to be the community's primary resource. Givers of strong advice, they are said to be the holders of cultural heritage and had witnessed, themselves, events such as this (or worse) in the past; these experiences put them in a unique position to know how to stop certain activities and provide guidance for those who seek it.

This comment about fires implicated other issues of entrenched violence in the community and substance abuse for which people are fighting to overcome. As different participants stood up and introduced themselves and their concern, each framed these issues (fires, language, violence) as symptoms of a much larger issue. A woman stands up and tells the group to remember 'the creativity and perseverance of residential school survivors and all the creative outlets we have.' It is at this moment that a silent truth is revealed: the legacy of residential schools is the *problem* facing the community. In the wake of this destructive colonial policy most participants are seeking solutions to community issues most of which are understood to trace back to the effect of residential schools. However, the identification of residential schools as a primary community problem does not fit within the *logic* and goals of the workshop but can be located within larger reconciliation discourses in Canada.

Reckoning and reconciliation

Where does this police workshop on crime prevention fit within larger discourses in Canada? On the one hand this is a workshop hosted by the police during a period of police practice transformation. In what could be seen as an era of neoliberal policing (Herbert, 2001; Stenson, 1993), practices have shifted from paternalistic policies to practices that require communities to become responsible for their own crime prevention. On the other hand, the workshop is being held during a time of 'national reconciliation,' a time in which church and state appear to be taking responsibility and being accountable for past deeds.

Seen this way, the workshop is steeped in rationalities of liberalism that have emerged at a specific moment *in* the politics of recognition requiring a richer analysis of the type of *work* taking place over what constitutes a community 'problem.' Held during the era of reconciliation, that presumes to heal colonial wounds, the workshop becomes a space in which police and community members must reckon with the legacy of residential schools as part of their collaboration on community problems. Reckoning in this space works otherwise to reconciliation, not to order and resolve but to disrupt, displace – to remind. The workshop serves as a discrete encounter in which police must reckon with the ongoing influence of residential schools (a legacy that is tied to the institution of policing).[11] Community problems once understood as vandalism, truancy, drug use, etc. are reordered and relationally positioned to the ongoing effect of residential schools. To better situate these practices, I will offer some texture and background on the macro-practices surrounding residential schools and the expectations of reconciliation.

Movement at the limits - politics of recognition

On Wednesday, 11 June 2008, the Prime Minister of Canada, Stephen Harper, appeared on live television. His rehearsed speech was a complicated official apology to the Aboriginal peoples of Canada on behalf of the government of Canada. As part of the highly publicized formal event, Harper delivered the apology from parliament before a group of witnesses including Aboriginal representatives. Daytime talk shows were interrupted by the Prime Minister who began his speech by tracing out the political genealogy of this historic act. The historicity of the apology, and the historicizing of the event(s), served as central elements in Harper's own choice of words.

'It is a sad chapter,' lamented the Prime Minister as he described the era of residential schools and the effects on Aboriginal peoples throughout Canada. Though apologetic, the metaphor of the chapter serves to incidentally indicate closure; a chapter, however sad, has a discrete beginning and end. As Harper outlined the ideology that informed practices and the legacy that endures the metaphor of the chapter was betrayed for it was not, and could not, be something that would close.

Colonial era, state-sponsored residential schools followed a transition in colonial administration from trade-focused relations to settlement-driven policies crafted to make room for settlers and railroad tracks alike.[12] These state-sponsored programs were meant to target the 'Indian problem' through massive projects of assimilation. From the imposition of schools for the children to laws that banned ceremonial practices, the governing ideologies of modernity mixed with liberal philosophy served to organize Aboriginal peoples into a pile of things outside of modernity; as objects that could not be accounted for in a colonial era governed by the logics of universality and individualism (Shewell, 2004).

To produce this massive educational institution committed to excising culture from each child was both a bureaucratic and religious undertaking. At first requested and later mandatory, the schools stripped children from their family homes with the goal of conditioning the young bodies to become laborers. As school attendance became mandatory in the 1920s and truancy a crime (Jack, 2006), enforcement of these colonial policies was often handled by the RCMP. Unlike the USA that closed most Indian boarding schools by the mid-1930s (Smith, 2005), Canada closed the last of its schools in the 1990s. The penitentiary-style form of education and assimilation became the loci for massive physical, sexual, and psychology abuse. Harper described a policy that was informed by an ideology that sought to 'kill the Indian in the child.'

The speech went on to detail the loss of life, the abuse suffered and the continued effect on individuals and communities. Harper spoke of the courage of those who have spoken up about their abuse and the many others who died before receiving a government apology. This was a formal recognition and laid the pavement upon which the apology stood.

'*Nous le regrettons.*' 'We are sorry,' Harper stated in back-to-back translations as he transitioned the tone of the speech to discuss the Indian Residential School Settlement Agreement that had began in September 2007. A central element of this $5 billion class action lawsuit was the reparations that were being settled with survivors of nearly five generations of residential school education alongside a national Truth and Reconciliation Commission (TRC) program. Harper offered that the TRC was a 'valuable chance to educate all Canadians' and that the result of the TRC would be a *stronger* Canada based on a better understanding of these events. Like so many other nations, Canada would translate 'apology' into a nation-building opportunity by framing the way in which Aboriginal peoples, and the nation, were to recognize the effect of residential school within a larger framework of reconciliation.

> The government recognizes that the absence of an apology has been an impediment to the healing and reconciliation. Therefore, on behalf of the government of Canada and all Canadians, I stand before you, in this chamber so central to our life as a country, to apologize to aboriginal peoples for Canada's role in the Indian residential schools system. To the approximately 80,000 living former students, and all the family members and communities, the government of Canada now recognizes that it was wrong to forcibly remove children from their homes and we apologize for having done this. (Federal Government of Canada, 2008)

For many there was a need to formally recognize the role of residential schools on the national stage. But it is a stage. Canada and Australia are the only states to apologize to the Aboriginal population about colonial programs; Canada the only to do so while concurrently engaged in a reparation program (that includes settlement payments to survivors of residential schools). But it is to see these as performances on a political stage. It is not to say that the performance does not serve a purpose but it is to call it a performance just the same. Just as the workshop becomes a productive space to understand a different notion of reckoning, so too does the apology serves as a productive space to reconsider the terms of recognition, justice-making, reconciliation.

The courtesy of recognizing

'Due recognition is not just a courtesy we owe people. It is a vital human need,' argues Charles Taylor (1995, p. 226) when discussing recognition as a politically charged, dialogical action that serves to construct identities – at times individual, and other times cultural (Taylor, 1994, 1995). In offering the apology, Harper mobilized recognition as a central object (manifested in an apology). In so doing, the apology was meant to facilitate reconciliation as part of the project to *move* the nation *forward* – out of the chapter, away from the events. That is towards a state of acceptable recognition and reconciliation. It is the move towards resolution. Recognition is alluring for what it may promise; however, it is important to press further and ask what recognition presumes and, in turn, what it demands in exchange.

Anthropologist Elizabeth Povinelli offers a critical examination of Australia's multiculturalism and the liberal practices of recognition in relationship to indigenous groups and individuals. Writing during a time of Australian nation reconciliation, she offers an intervention in the presumptions of recognition:

> Before we can develop a 'critical theory of recognition,' or politics of redistribution and capabilities, we need to understand better the cunning of recognition; its intercalation of the politics of culture with the culture of capital. We need to puzzle over the simple question: What is the nation recognizing, capital commodifying, and the court trying to save from the breach of history when difference is recognized? (Povinelli, 2002, p. 17)

Critically, Povinelli asks, what is the nation recognizing to save from the breach of history? What stories must be accounted for when difference is recognized? Povenelli's work serves to remind the reader of the 'impossible demand' placed upon indigenous people who must fit within a particular vision of multiculturalism such that diversity is achieved but does not operate in excess of what the state is *willing to recognize*.

Critical theorist Nancy Fraser speaks of the 'problem of recognition' when she points out that identity-based politics can undermine redistribution (2000). Her work focuses on the need for different groups (class, race, ethnic, gender, sexuality, etc.) to articulate claims that do not privilege identity politics over the need for wider redistribution of resources. Fraser's call for wider redistribution makes an important intervention in the privileging of one claim over another but also reveals that each of these groups must advocate to a power broker, such as the state. Fraser's work is an important intervention in that she is calling for wider coalitions of advocacy and activism. But faces the ultimate challenge of petitioning for recognition; asking for the state to willingly recognize claims.

These three approaches (Taylor, Povinelli, Fraser) to recognition can reveal a troubled terrain. Whereas Taylor offers it as a vital human need, and Fraser cautions that claims must be properly conceived to ensure better redistribution, Povinelli reminds the reader that the state remains the broker and holds the power *to* recognize. What then does it mean to be recognized, to properly articulate the claim and then to wait until it is recognized? In the case of the apology in Canada, a representative of the state offered a calculated apology that spoke about the need to learn from and move beyond the legacy of the residential school. But in so doing, the apology set the frame and the boundary of what constituted the offense and what the state was willing to do with regards of redistribution. The apology was meant to frame (and limit) the admission of guilt and then to instigate movement, a step forward, toward reconciliation. Here the apology acts as a frame, as one step in a planned series of moves expected to yield reconciliation. And the state is not alone in placing apologies within larger narratives and expectations of movement such that a successful apology is expected to do a certain amount of work within the project of reconciliation.

Communication theorist Adina Abadi reviews the literature on apologies and produces a model upon which to understand the success and failure of public apologies (1990). For Abadi an apology, as a speech act, can be broken up into constitutive parts including such elements as: acknowledging responsibility, partial responsibility, with/without renunciation, with/without promise to refrain, with/without offer of amends etc. This review raises questions about the presumption to universality: if the apology does acknowledge responsibility, and renounces the act with a promise to offer amends it is understood that this type of apology will produce a certain a/effect. For example, viewed as sincere it will be better accepted, etc. In some respects this disarticulation of the apology into central elements can also be found in the work of sociologist Nicholas Tavuchis who also cautions that the apology delivered too early or too late can lose its ability to hold sway (Tavuchis, 1991). Bound up in these two pieces is what I see as a teleological expectation of apologies that is both problematic and, arguably, untenable.

The role of acknowledgment, what some call the 'moral apology' (Brooks, 2006; Govier & Verwoerd, 2002), is central to reconciliation. This argument is highlighted in the work of Govier and Verwoerd (2002). However, folded into this formulation is that, if delivered correctly, the apology brings about an expectation that the oppressed will: (1) hear and accept the apology, and then (2) move towards reconciling with their oppressor. This mode of recognition and formulation produces a troubling situation in which the state becomes a doubled entity such that it is both a (past) agent of oppression *and* (present) agent of healing.

From Harper's speech we are given movement: 'towards healing, reconciliation and resolution.' Within Harper's own framework, the state mobilizes healing through the practice of recognition (as delivered in the apology) that will bring about (in this order) reconciliation and resolution. At the center of which appears a promise of sorts: with the apology there can then come healing, reconciliation, and resolution. Govier and Verwoerd pick up on this notion of promise when they write: 'The promise is that a wholehearted apology, followed up with proper commitment to reform and practical amends, can provide a major initial step toward restoring injured relationships' (2002, p. 79). Although there is a promise of a first step in restoring relationships, there is much work that must be done to enact the process. And it is in the waiting, for the promise to materialize, for the apology to come, for the reparations to start that alternate modalities emerge.

Without the compulsion to close

In *Magic Weapons: Aboriginal Writers Remaking Community after Residential Schools*, Sam McKegney provides a literary review of Aboriginal narratives of survival (of residential schools) to focus on the role of narration and storytelling as a weapon against state frameworks. He writes:

> Through their writings, Native authors imagine alternative ideological and political horizons for Indigenous communities and individuals, loosening the neo-colonial bonds of non-Native authority and mapping out possible paths to empowerment and healing that reinvigorate traditional knowledges while refusing to rely solely on the structures of governmental power ... The purpose of *Magic Weapons* has been to analyze how the autonomous incarnations of residential school survival narratives, while intimately connected to individual understandings of historical reality, encourage new strategies for empowerment that seek to emancipate Indigenous peoples from the yoke of acculturative history. (McKegney, 2007, p. 180)

The use of storytelling stands central in many such projects in Canada (Jack, 2006; McKegney, 2007; Oskiniko & Manuel, 1998) and produces a complicated counter-narrative that includes admissions of the good that residential school did for some children alongside revelations of the horrors suffered by others. Many narratives also serve to illustrate the insidious techniques and practices of institutionalized racism. The legacy of colonial ideology persists in Canada as the ideas that produced residential schools continue to inform contemporary racism that infects the country:

> Canadians as a rule have much to say and lament about Indian welfare dependency but little to offer in the way of solutions. Most rely on stock answers: Indians are lazy, welfare has made them lazy, they have to stop drinking, they should get a job, they should leave the reserve – in short, they should be like us. (Shewell, 2004, p. 3)

Shewell points to the process of assimilation that continues to take place in Canada. Seen this way, grand programs of reconciliation may seem less appealing over smaller projects; opportunities for a different way to frame these experiences and, perhaps, without the compulsion to close. This mode might appeal to those who do not agree to operate within the terms of recognition.

Alternate practices can take place in unexpected locations when the opportunity presents itself. The crime prevention workshop, itself located within the reconciliation project, may be one such location. Because the police role in residential schools is not inconsequential – nor forgotten – the workshop is involved in overlapping networks of associations and presents an opportunity for residents to engage in different conversations about residential schools. In this strange space that bring residents and police together, community members seize the opportunity to frame community problems in relationship to the historical effects of residential schools. Importantly, if residential schools are a fundamental issue, then to name them implicates the RCMP and their role in the schools. To name them as central, as specifically historical problems that demand collaboration, resets the terms of the workshop transforming it into a space in which residential schools must be reckoned with. It is not to say that RCMP were not aware of the legacy of residential schools, but it is to say that the terms of the conversation are shifting.

Driving down an isolated stretch of highway. It is a cold winter night and we are passing the time with idle chat about police practices and patrolling the highway in remote locations. 'You know you can't talk about the RCMP without talking about Aboriginal and First Nations policing,' he explained to me the unique style of police work that takes place in these communities where the RCMP are required to police but always operate as outsiders, with a link to the state's colonial past. He turns to me and, despite darkness and slippery roads, holds his stare for a moment. 'We used to be the truancy officers,' he nods to me, and I nod back. He refers to truancy officers for the residential schools. When it was law to attend, RCMP members were required to go to the reserves and ensure children were at school (under threat of arrest for parents that resisted). His stare returns to the road ahead and soon we speak about the challenges of learning new radar techniques.

To reckon with

In the workshop, the facilitator is tasked to instruct the community on the history of police work, explain the role of collaboration and partnerships in policing as central elements of successful crime prevention projects, and assist participants to isolate and identify discrete community problems that the participants can work on. However, the context and conditions under which these workshops take place undermines the distinction between small and large community problems. Evidenced through the group introductions, as participants outlined their reasons for attending the workshop, there really did not exist any *small* issues in the community that could be compartmentalized and reduced to facilitate this approach to policing. However, rather than classifying this as simple, I want to revisit the workshop introductions to see if something else is taking place.

Bob's job as the facilitator was to listen for community problems, compartmentalize them, and help the group distill all the problems into a short list. By the second day the participants would 'vote' on the issues which would help them prioritize which problems they would work on as a group. From all the problems listed the vote would reveal a top five list of issues to which working groups would be assigned. During the group introduction I could see Bob make notes to himself as he attempted to extract a problem from each person's narrative. As he paraphrased at times between speakers his inclination was to distill the various stories into discrete police categories – problems at the boardwalk would be read back to the group as vandalism, in which the boardwalk as the example and discussions about fires being set in the community were described as 'arson.' However, pressing these personal events into the codified language of property crime was extremely problematic. And it was only through narrative, through introductions, that the language of policing was challenged and terms of the discussion shifted.

Take for example the issue of graveyard desecration. From a policing perspective this would be listed as an act of vandalism – tipping gravestones and/or tossing gravestones into the ocean – and within the logic of the workshop a committee could think about how to halt vandalism (more generally) through a wide range of strategies. But for local community members, this was not a *simple issue* of vandalism. For many, the acts at the graveyard were part of a much larger web of problems. To handle the vandalism would require a series of actions including: outreaching to elders to speak to youth about the need to respect ancestors and for the community to work together to heal the violence this type of action was having upon *all* the members of the community.

One young man stood up and spoke about the actions at the graveyard and the type of psychic violence it produced in the community. The seventh-grade student spoke of the fear residents have about going out at night and alluded to the ways in which these acts serve to scratch at old scars. Pressing together the graveyard desecration and other acts at the boardwalk. '*Every week*,' his voice pinched, people would tear up part of the boardwalk that surrounds the graveyard and toss the wooden planks – occasionally into the ocean, other times alongside the pathway. Every week people would go down to the small neighboring island and attempt to fix the damage. There was fatigue in his small body, anxiety in his voice, as he described the weekly occurrence. Here, the acts were not vandalism – an act upon property (a property crime) – but were seen as an act upon residents which were part of a much deeper-seeded set of problems in the community.

'We know this is not sustainable, to have to go and fix the boardwalk each week. So what can we do about that?' Bob summarized his understanding of the situation. But these were not concerns about the Boardwalk, just as property damage was not the fundamental concern about the fires.

A man stands up in the corner of the room and introduces himself as the Chief of the Fire Department. There are smiles and nods. He begins to speak of the fires that happened the previous summer, when many buildings were 'lit up'; he then speaks of a specific fire. He explains to the group that as volunteer firemen, they arrived focused on containing the fire in the older house. As they worked on containment they made the horrific discovery that there was a person inside the burning building. The emergency call went out to send help from the mainland – a survivor would need to be taken from the small island by helicopter to the regional hospital. As the skeleton of the smoldering building coughed up its final plumes of smoke, the firemen sat with the man, as he succumbed to his injuries.

The fireman explains he is attending the meeting because of these issues in the community. Swallowing hard to contain tears he spoke of the intimacies of that night; of realizing that someone was on fire in the building, of sitting with a man who realized he was going to die and watching an elder, forced into a debilitating addiction for reasons that span a lifetime, be caught on fire because he was too intoxicated to detect the fire in time; of an elder dying because 'kids were bored' in the community. The fireman ends his introduction with a few words about the good work he hopes will come of the workshop. But as he sits down and I look around the room I can see the translations that continue to take place as Bob attempts to reconcile the narrative to a 'problem' in the community. For many of the police in the room, the workshop is about crime prevention and assigning community responsibility to local issues. But during this story, I watch one of the local officers and I can see it is about something else – something that reaches far beyond arson. I see him mourn with other community members the event of that summer night that echo and resonates through spring. The workshop, for him, is not about assigning responsibility to the community but perhaps something more.

I watch him as he listens to rest of the introductions and I begin to think about the ways in which problems are articulated often down one of two paths: violence and/or addiction all of which are said to be directly linked to the fall-out of residential schools. The officer does not take notes, but nods. These issues cannot be solved in an afternoon but the participants were willing to put them on the table, to share. Sharing in a room, the legacy of colonial practices in front of police officers who have a relationship to this past – it is to reckon with these practices, these problems. This is to open wounds that continue to infect the community. Most of the problems raised in the introductions, as articulated by participants, fall under broad categories related to cultural heritage, abuse and healing – all three are understood to have direct lineage to residential schools. In this meeting, community members and police each have a relationship to residential schools both with defined roles during this era.

Bob continues to make his list and paraphrase individuals. Later that day the lists will go up on the wall and participants will be asked to vote – to prioritize the issues that need to be 'resolved' in the community. The list is long expanded such that it could include everything from local bootleggers to the need to support the annual inter-tribal basketball competition. But during the introduction, a vast network of association bound together narratives of shared concern. Each story stitched individuals together and affirmed the larger belief in the legacy of residential schools. Though the reasons for participating might appear divergent – vandalism, employment, substance abuse, sexual abuse, fisheries and treaty settlements, need for after-school programs, more counseling services, language and cultural heritage and bullying programs – taken together they present a mosaic of co-constituting concerns that everyone understood relationally and in direct conversation with residential schools and colonial practices.

'We are two hours off schedule,' Bob whispers to me during the first nutrition break/coffee break as I collect a homemade muffin and coffee. After a quick break for fresh air, I wander back into the community center I see one of the local police officers making quick steps toward Bob. Something is about to transpire. I weave through the crowd quickly. As I walk up, I hear Bob reiterate his concern about the schedule. Bob tries to articulate Janice's strong endorsement about the need for an entire go around and concedes that it put them off schedule. 'It had to happen,' the local officer intervenes and outlines all of the prominent members of the tribe and tribal council who were present. In hushed tones he indicates their participation had to be publicly recognized in this group and then turns his comments to other elements of the workshop that had to be changed in order to accommodate local needs.

The rest of the morning session is dedicated to 'risk and protective' factors as participants are instructed about risk by reviewing a series of 'profiles' of fictive youth. The walls will later fill with the problems of the community and each member will be given five small flags to vote. The second day is to be devoted to problem solving techniques and group work on how to *solve* the community problems. From enormous lists just five issues would be the focus and the group was divided into teams that each would come up with strategies, goals, and deadlines to tackle each issue. The legacy of residential schools had many votes cast in small colorful post-it flags (Figure 3). It would be one of the issues the community would tackle.

I was told later, at the regional police office that everyone was excited when the workshop concluded and projects were underway. Police reported it locally and regionally as a raving success – a model community that was involved in the workshop from beginning to end (Figure 4). However, when I visited the small community a few months later I was told that the community meetings stopped after the workshop. I talked to the fireman who said he did not think the meetings would take place again but that he thought the workshop was a 'good idea.'

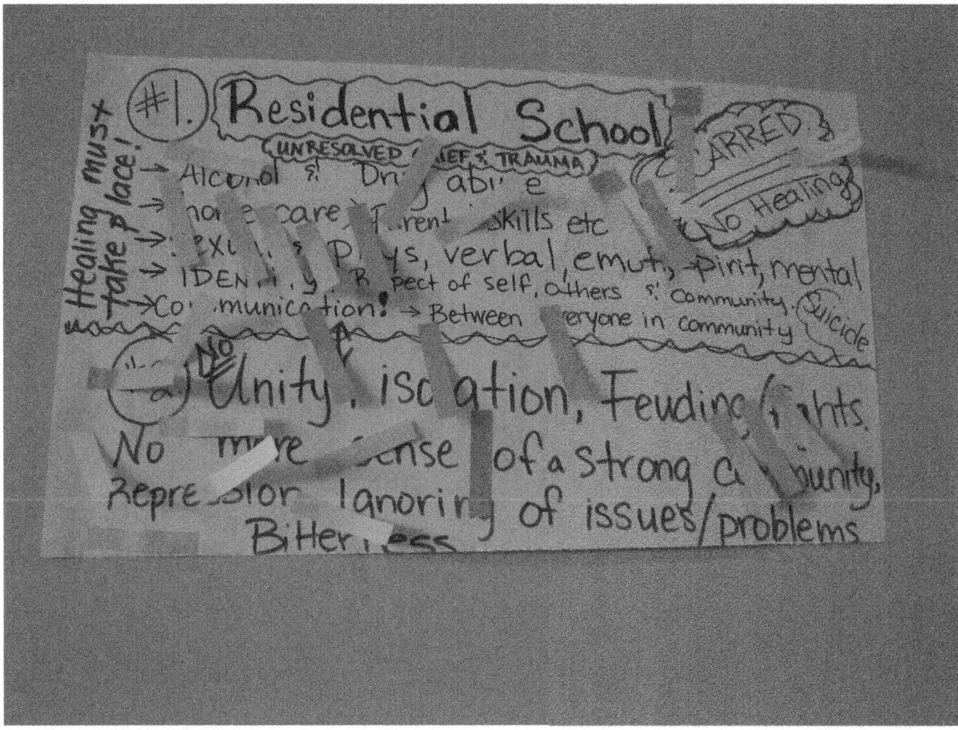

Figure 3. After groups identify a series of problems in the community, participants vote with small sticky flags. These 'votes' are then counted up, and the top four or five community problems are identified. The workshop concludes with committees creating plans to address these issues and presenting their plans to the entire workshop. Seen here, residential schools were voted the number 1 problem to be reckoned with.

So did the workshop *work*? The simple answer might be yes.

Each workshop is *doing* a lot of work – even if it was not the work originally imagined. At the RCMP level the workshop serves to illustrate (back to the RCMP and its members) the ways in which regional resources can be used to support small communities. At the local level the workshop is meant to bring together a small number of committed community members to talk about ways for police and community to collaborate. The first piece of work this project does is to reveal the ways in which the terms of collaboration are being radically redefined in practice. In this workshop, a facilitator stands before the community and, alongside local police officers, tells the community: the police are not in charge of *your* problems. This is a severe message, it is counter-intuitive in many respects as individuals in Canada have been trained and conditioned in many ways to understand police as problem solvers. The message now is that *you*, workshop participants/community members, must become your own problem solvers. In this way the tide has changed, this is not 'community policing' as usual, as police are not simply asking the public to *join* them in helping to police (Brunschot, 2003; Cattelino, 2004; Chesluk, 2004; Das & Lab, 2003; Gianakis & Davis, 1998; Livingston, 1997; Pérez, 2008; Reed, 1999; Tilley, 2005), but rather are telling the public what they are *no longer willing* to police. This is particular to Canada, and is a marked shift in practice over the past decade.

Figure 4. Following the workshop, the student participants created posters to represent the top four issues in the community. The posters were hung in the hallway of the school for months following.

From another vantage point, however, local residents enter into the workshop with varying understandings of the goals, but upon entering engage in a tacit agreement that they are willing to listen and perhaps work with the police. And, despite the message that police are not the exclusive 'owners' (or solvers) of community problems, local police officers attend the meeting and listen to the community members articulate local problems as part of a longer history and police engage in these dialogues. Indeed, the workshop, the terms of the dialogue, shifted when community members rewrote the terms of the workshop indicating more at stake in this conversation about crime prevention – there was more to reckon with.

One participant explained that the workshop allowed it 'to be said,' that the long introduction served as a time to share experiences and stories and in so doing, not everything but many things were said. She is quick to caution that no one spoke about sexual violence but implies that with visitors in the room this conversation would not happen. In a community trying to overcome the effects of residential schools, the schools are understood to be the base that produced the violence and crime; the workshop allowed individuals to reckon with this legacy. This was the labor and *work*. In this way the workshop was transformed from a diagnostics space in which crime could be cured in the community to a space of reckoning in which the past had to be wrested with to understand what challenges the community was currently facing. So, in many respects, the workshop *works*; often producing incredible exhaustion for participants as police and community members attempt to reckon with residential schools in the attempt to account for – to produce consistent – a story about the problems that face a particular community.

This article is not arguing that these workshops serve to replace the formal reconciliation processes taking place in Canada – no more so than it is arguing that these workshops serve to reconcile colonial actions. Rather, this article reveals the ways in which a police-community workshop served to open up a dialogue and discussion about what are understood to be the material effects of residential schools. Through situated practice, the workshop was transformed into a different type of *work* space that required all parties to reckon with the past – to reckon with a shared history of an institution and group of people. It facilitated conversations about the past that might not have otherwise taken place and offers a space between the steps and promises of reconciliation. As these and other modes of policing are implemented in different communities it is important to consider how this changes the framework and understanding of what constitutes police work and the conditions under which problems can be policed.

Acknowledgments

This material is based upon work supported by the National Science Foundation under Grant No. 0819627 along with generous support of the Pacific Rim Research Program and the Canadian Embassy. I would like to thank all the officers and staff of the RCMP as well as the community members who shared their time and experiences and made my research possible. I would also like to thank my advisors Joe Dumit, Marisol de la Cadena, Patrick Carroll, and Alan Klima as well as Darryl Plecas for his support and guidance. I am indebted to Chris Kortright, Jieun Lee, Gowoon Noh, and Michael Stewart as well for reading and commenting on earlier drafts along with the editors of this volume and the anonymous reviewers for their helpful comments.

Notes

1. Michelle Stewart is a doctoral candidate at the University of California Davis. Michelle conducted ethnographic fieldwork with police in Canada to investigate the ways in which transnational policing practices are articulated locally through specific training practices. She discusses how these training practices act to reshape relationships between police and public and, in turn, reformulate definitions and expectations of: police officers, community members, crime and criminal activity.
2. Excerpt taken from Canadian Prime Minister Stephen Harper's national apology (Federal Government of Canada, 2008) to Aboriginal peoples for residential schools in Canada.
3. Royal Canadian Mounted Police are the federal police force for the nation and are the most common form of police service in most communities.
4. The workshop includes a multi-module lesson plan that seeks to instruct participants on the history of RCMP practices, offers instruction on emerging police theory including crime prevention through social development and environmental design alongside skills building projects directed toward problem solving and risk management.
5. I would argue the crime prevention workshop (this mode of policing in Canada) operates at the limits community-oriented policing as it is involved in a new production of accountability.
6. This type of policing is the focus of my larger dissertation on transnational police training and practices.
7. RCMP detachments are the term used for local RCMP police stations.
8. The process of selecting the top issues in the community involves each of the small groups in the workshop brainstorming key issues and then presenting their 'top five'

concerns to the larger group. These different issues are placed onto large 'post-it' notes and hung up on the wall. During the breaks all the participants are given a limited number of little sticky flags that they use to vote with. After everyone has voted the flag are counted up and the end result of the 'election' is the selection of four to five key issues. The workshop concludes with the formulation of working groups that draw up plans to address the issue.

9. All names appearing in this text are pseudonyms.
10. It is later explained to me by both the principal and another teacher that it is difficult to keep a regular staff at the school. Staff are paid well by the community but many do not stay on for long. Some, I am told, take stress-relief within the opening months of this position. Still others struggle to stay committed to teaching in the community where school attendance is remarkably low and isolation becomes a central complaint.
11. It is important to note that RCMP officers were often used to enforce the state's laws surrounding residential schools.
12. French Recollects and Jesuits administered early residential schools.

References

Abadi, A. (1990). The speech act of apology in political life. *Journal of Pragmatics, 14*, 467–487.

Brooks, RL. (2006). The new patriotism and apology for slavery. In E. Barkan & A. Karn (Eds.), *Taking wrongs seriously: Apologies and reconciliation* (pp. 213–233). Stanford, CA: Stanford University Press.

Brunschot, E.G.V. (2003). Community policing and 'John Schools.' *Canadian Review of Sociology and Anthropology, 40*, 215–232.

Bullock, K., Erol, R., & Tilley, N. (2006). *Problem-oriented policing and partnerships: Implementing an evidence-based approach to crime reduction.* Portland, OR: Willan Publishing.

Burnett, E. (2007). Crime analysis reporting and mapping for small agencies. *FBI Law Enforcement Bulletin, 76*, 15–22.

Cattelino, J. (2004). The difference citizenship makes: Civilian crime prevention in the lower east side. *PoLAR, 27*, 114–137.

Chesluk, B. (2004). Visible signs of a city out of control: Community policing in New York. *Cultural Anthropology, 19*, 250–275.

Das, D.K., & Lab, S.P. (2003). *International perspectives on community policing and crime prevention.* Upper Saddle River, NJ: Prentice-Hall.

Everson, S. (2003). Repeat victimisation and prolific offending: Chance or choice? *International Journal of Police Science & Management, 5*, 180–194.

Federal Government of Canada. (2008). *Prime Minister Stephen Harper's Statement of Apology.* Ottawa: Author.

Fraser, N. (2000). Rethinking recognition. *New Left Review, 3*, 107–120.

Gianakis, G.A., & Davis, J., III. (1998). Reinventing or repackaging public service? The case of community-oriented policing. *Public Administration Review, 58*, 485–498.

Govier, T., & Verwoerd, W. (2002). The promise and pitfalls of apology. *Journal of Social Philosophy, 33*, 67–82.

Haraway, D. (1988). Situated knowledges: The science question in feminism and the privilege of partial perspective. *Feminist Studies, 14*, 575–599.

Herbert, S. (2001). Policing the contemporary city: Fixing broken windows or shoring up neoliberalism? *Theoretical Criminology, 5*, 445–466.

Jack, A. (Ed.). (2006). *Behind closed doors: Stories from the Kamloops Indian Residential School.* Kamloops: Secwepemc Cultural Education Society.

Livingston, D. (1997). Police discretion and the quality of life in public places: Courts, communities, and the new policing. *Columbia Law Review, 97*, 551–672.

Mawby, R.C., & Worrall, A. (2004). 'Polibation' revisited: Policing, probation and prolific offender projects. *International Journal of Police Science & Management, 6*, 63–73.

McKegney, S. (2007). *Magic weapons: Aboriginal writers remaking the community after residential schools.* Manitoba: University of Manitoba.

Nelson, D.M. (2009). *Reckoning: The ends of war in Guatemala.* Durham, NC: Duke University Press.

Oskiniko, L.L., & Manuel, V. (1998). *Two plays about residential school.* Vancouver: Living Traditions.

Pérez, R.L. (2008). The misunderstanding of Mexican community life in urban apartment space: A case study in applied anthropology and community policing. *City & Society, 18*, 232–259.

Povinelli, E.A. (2002). *The cunning of recognition: Indigenous alterities and the making of Australian multiculturalism.* Durham, NC: Duke University Press.

Reed, W. (1999). *The politics of community policing: The case of Seattle.* New York: Garland Publishing.

Shewell, H. (2004). *'Enough to keep them alive': Indian welfare in Canada, 1873–1965.* Toronto: University of Toronto Press.

Smith, A. (2005). *Conquest: Sexual violence and American Indian genocide.* Cambridge, MA: South End Press.

Stenson, K. (1993). Community policing as a governmental technology. *Economy and Society, 22*, 373–389.

Tavuchis, N. (1991). *Mea Culpa: A sociology of apology and reconciliation.* Stanford, CA: Stanford University Press.

Taylor, C. (Ed.). (1994). *Multiculturalism: Examining the politics of recognition.* Princeton, NJ: Princeton University Press.

Taylor, C. (1995). *Philosophical arguments.* Cambridge, MA: Harvard University Press.

Tilley, N. (Ed.). (2005). *Handbook of crime prevention and community safety.* Portland, OR: Willan Publishing.

The Shanti Sena 'peace center' and the non-policing of an anarchist temporary autonomous zone: Rainbow Family peacekeeping strategies

Michael I. Niman

Communications Department, Buffalo State College, Bishop Hall 210, 1300 Elmwood Avenue, Buffalo, NY 14222, USA

This article utilizes ethnographic methods and government documents to examine the self-policing and peacekeeping strategies of the Rainbow Family, a non-violent acephalous intentional community that holds massive weeklong gatherings around the globe. It is a case study that examines the efficacy of these methods, comparing them to those traditional police agencies employ under similar conditions. It contextualizes these strategies by examining other utopian and anarchist communities and movements such as Critical Mass bike rides. This study demonstrates how smiling, chanting, listening, social pressure, and social capital all play into forming a more effective and less violent approach toward peacekeeping.

Introduction

This article examines the self-policing and peacekeeping strategies that the Rainbow Family of Living Light employs at its annual weeklong Gatherings of up to 30,000 people. Rather than maintaining selective membership or admittance rules that would make these Gatherings violence-free, the Family instead maintains an open-admissions policy and, as part of its healing mission, has consciously reached out to violent and disruptive people. Hence, its Gatherings are not simply free of violence but actively apply non-violent conflict resolution strategies to confront and harmonize violent behavior. In this way, the Gatherings are actively non-violent rather than passively non-violent. Rainbow Family members who confront violence become what the Family terms, 'Shanti Sena.' Their tactics have proven, over the Family's 38-year history, to be more effective than traditional police tactics in defusing violent situations and gaining compliance with group norms and values. This article examines the efficacy of Shanti Sena tactics and related Rainbow Family survival strategies, while comparing them to the less effective compliance tactics that traditional police agencies employ at and near Rainbow Gatherings.

Rainbow Family background

Since 1972, the Rainbow Family of Living Light, an acephalous nonhierarchical nomadic society, has been holding large temporary gatherings in remote forests around the world to pray for world peace and to create a model of a functioning utopian society. Their goal is to reform the mainstream society that birthed them, which they call 'Babylon.[1]' They also term their Gatherings as 'healing,' aiming to provide a healthy supportive atmosphere for all who come. What began as an American movement morphed into a global phenomenon in the 1980s with Rainbow Gatherings now on every continent except Antarctica. The Gatherings form what anarchist theorist Hakim Bey terms a temporary autonomous zone, or TAZ (Bey, 1991, pp. 100–101), liberating time rather than a permanent space. For the duration of the Gathering,[2] the Rainbows seek to celebrate an autonomous culture independent of Babylon. During that liberated time, their utopian experiment plays out.

The Rainbows see their gatherings of up to 30,000 people, led by an all-inclusive consensus council, as small-scale actualizations of a utopian vision encompassing nonviolence, egalitarianism, sustainability, and an anarchist vision of a full participation democracy. While Rainbows grapple with issues such as what actually constitutes environmental sustainability and what role governing councils should play at Gatherings, they have, since their inception, always been united behind a defining ethos of nonviolence. Today's international Rainbow Family has a four-decade-long history as a 'peaceable people' (cf. Amster, 2003, p. 17; Dentan, 1992, 1994; Niman, 1991, 1997; Solnit, 2009, pp. 295–299).

From their onset, Rainbow Family Councils reaffirmed the Family's mission to not only practice nonviolence but also actively promote such nonviolence in the larger world by establishing the Gatherings as models of peaceful coexistence, successfully employing nonviolent conflict resolution strategies when engaging violence and potentially violent situations. Rainbows view 'Babylonian' policing models as inherently violent, either directly employing violence or threatening violence. Hence, in order to keep the Gatherings nonviolent, Rainbows avoid calling in traditional armed police agencies, even when confronting violent provocations.

Field testing non-violence in an all-inclusive society

The Rainbow Family's commitment to nonviolence and the avoidance of requesting aid from violent police agencies are not unique. What sets the Family apart, however, from most other nonviolent utopian groups is their dual commitments to nonviolence and open membership. To the Rainbows, anyone who shows up at a Gathering is a Family member. Since the Family is a subculture born of Babylon, engulfed in Babylon, and with open fluid borders between its Gatherings and Babylon, Rainbows are quick to remind visitors that what is 'out there' in Babylon is also 'in here' at the Gatherings. Over the years, rapists, child predators, muggers, thieves, and violent drunks have visited Rainbow Gatherings. In describing these visitors, I'm careful not to use terms like 'unwelcome guests,' because Rainbow tradition welcomes everyone to the Gatherings, especially those who clearly need to be healed. In this respect, the Family is following anarcho-pacifist ideals outlined in 1877 by Peter Kropotkin (2002[1877]), who argued that membership in a society that offers a simple and friendly helping hand is far more effective than a prison or mental institution in deterring or reversing anti-social behavior, which he said stemmed from societal alienation. He writes:

> Today we live too isolated. Private property has led us to an egotistic individualism in all our mutual relations. We know one another only slightly; our points of contact are too rare. But we have seen in history examples of a communal life which is more intimately bound together ... By force of circumstances they must aid one another materially and morally. (Kropotkin, 2002[1877], p. 233)

Kropotkin argued that modern industrial society was alienating people from that 'original community' and causing violent anti-social behaviors. He saw a Rainbow Family-like structure as the antidote:

> A new family, based on community of aspirations will take its [the original community's] place. In this family people will be obliged to know one another, to aid one another and to lean on one another for moral support on every occasion. And this mutual prop will prevent the great number of anti-social acts which we see today. (Kropotkin, 2002[1877], pp. 233–234)

Like the nineteenth-century Belgian peasant village of Gheel,[3] cited by Kropotkin for admonishing society to 'Send us your insane. We will give them absolute freedom,' (Kropotkin, 2002[1877], p. 234) the Rainbows have likewise opened their community to people who they see as 'needing healing.' Rainbows argue that this modern-day emulation of Gheel sets the family apart from Babylonian authorities who confront violence with more of the same violence, feeding a hopeless cycle. Like the residents of Gheel, Rainbows confront violence with peace and love, difficult as that sometimes may be. Twenty years ago, Joseph Schwartzbaum, an elderly Jewish concentration camp survivor who regularly attended Gatherings, explained to me:

> If you fight evil with evil, you are acting evil. If you fight, kill the killer, kill, kill, it's a constant killing so we are caught in a process of killing. So violence can never bring peace, hatred can never bring love, peace can bring peace. (Niman, 1997, p. 115)

The Rainbow Family's open-admissions policies have given the Family something that, for a nonviolent culture, is an embarrassing anomaly – a violent ghetto. 'Wet' and often violent drunks attend Gatherings, but usually confine themselves to the Family's 'A-Camp' (the A is for alcohol), a fixture unique to US Gatherings. A-Camp, which is always located at the perimeter of the Gathering, serves as the last stop in Babylon before entering the nonviolent Rainbow world. For many Rainbows, the disruptive antics at A-Camp (cf. Grant, 2003, pp. 203–231) are too much to bear, hence they stopped attending Gatherings. Other Rainbows, however, argue that it is the presence of A-Camp that makes the Gatherings truly nonviolent. The logic goes like this: While other historic utopias have been nonviolent, the existence of the violent A-Camp makes the Rainbows unique among historic utopias, giving them the opportunity to not just preach nonviolence to a nonviolent population, but to actively confront violence. Hence, in the face of real-time violence, Rainbows have the opportunity to actualize their rhetorical commitment to nonviolence and to demonstrate the real-world practicality of nonviolent conflict resolution strategies (cf. Niman, 1997, pp. 126–129; Niman, 2011, Epilogue Part 1).

Over the decades, A-Camp has served not only as a field test for nonviolence but has also served the Family's healing mission, acting as a conduit to recruit violent self-destructive alcoholics into the Family. While the Family's overall success rate in helping A-Campers overcome their addictions is low, A-Camp has been a conduit for some alcoholics to overcome their addictions and move into the Gathering proper. Those who have made the transition often prove to be among the Family's most energetic and committed volunteers. To Rainbows, who call the Gathering, 'home,' being at A-Camp is 'almost home.' They see the fact that A-Campers travel great distances to be nearly home as hopeful and indicative of a desire for healing. A-Camp represents the type of violent group that peaceful movements and communities in the USA have traditionally failed to effectively reach out to. According to peace studies anthropologist Robert Knox Dentan, 'None of these peace groups has recruited successfully among … the people whose lives are most painfully disrupted by violence.' Hence, he explains, 'Pacifist ideals that apply only to those already fairly safe from violence are not going to transform society' (1994, p. 95). The Rainbows have maintained an open gateway between A-Camp and the peaceful nurturing Gatherings. Those who have successfully transcended that boundary have found something akin to the healing community that Kropotkin describes and, hence, experienced a life-changing transformation.

Shanti Sena: participatory policing

While Kropotkin envisioned an egalitarian utopia where 'anti-social acts need not be feared in a society of equals,' he admitted that there will be 'those individuals with evil tendencies whom existing society will pass on to us …' His ideal community, he believed, would prevent such people from exercising these tendencies 'quite efficiently by the solidarity of all members of the community against such aggressors' (2002[1877], p. 235). This ideal, in essence, is the blueprint for what Rainbows call, Shanti Sena, from the Sanskrit phrase that translates roughly as 'peace center.' Unlike with a traditional police force, you do not *call* the Shanti Sena when you see a problem, you *become* the Shanti Sena. In theory, *all* Rainbows are Shanti Sena reserves waiting to self-activate, and, hence, should be ready to intercede as needed, eliminating the need for an organized security force.

Rainbow-style voluntary policing is not uncommon among groups forming temporary autonomous zones. Critical Mass urban bicycle rides, which create mobile TAZs,[4] have their own version of Shanti Sena, which they call, 'corkers.' Corkers are ride participants who 'leave the flow of the ride for a while' and stop, essentially acting as a traffic cop, 'in calm posture, a few feet from the front of stopped cars which would otherwise enter an intersection in use by Critical Mass' (Carlsson, 2002, p. 232; McClusky, 2003, 2004). Like Shanti Sena, ordinary people emerge from the general population as corkers when they see a need for a police-like task, in this case, an 'uncorked' intersection that presents the threat of a car–bike collision. Unlike traditional police, however, their authority stems not from a badge, but from 'smiles and eye contact' made with motorists (McClusky, 2003, 2004).

Shanti Sena, too, use smiles and eye contact, as well as friendly touch, when appropriate. When such tools alone cannot defuse a potentially violent situation, Shanti Sena often employ an 'Om circle,'[5] which consists of a circle of peacekeepers holding hands and chanting the harmonic syllable 'Ommmmmm.'[6] Rainbows use the non-dictionary verb 'Omming' to describe the practice of forming Om circles around agitated or threatening people. Recognizing an Om circle as non-threatening and harmonizing, however, is often a learned cultural trait. Those unfamiliar with the practice can see the circle as threatening – especially if they do not realize that they can walk right through and beyond it. And there is an argument among Rainbows that it can be coercive, if not applied gently. Even so, Rainbows consider the circles as 'nonviolent,' since, they explain, the key to an effective Om circle is love. Showing love, according to Rainbow tradition, is the best way to diffuse violent situations. Once the circle soothes a tense situation, the remaining conflict can be mediated with an impromptu council, where social pressure either shames belligerent parties into compromise or where balance can be restored to human relationships through mutual listening and sharing. Such circles follow an ancient social script common among nonhierarchical tribal groups (cf. Dentan, 2008, pp. 144–145; Pepinsky, 2000, pp. 177–178). These Shanti Sena Councils, like Om circles, must be loving, since the idea behind them is to nurture upset people with the hope that they will quickly see the futility of their anger, rather than see the council or circle as something to escape or rebel against. This love patrol is the antithesis of the Babylonian norm of an armed squadron of police or a court with the authority to jail or kill its charges.

Shanti Sena tactics work, in large part, because the Shanti Sena is not an alien occupation force, like suburb-dwelling police officers patrolling an inner-city community. Shanti Sena are first and foremost Rainbow Family members, usually driven by that kinship identification to volunteer for Shanti Sena duty. They are acquainted with and often recognized by members of their own Rainbow community. Such mutual familiarity of peacekeepers with their community, and of community members with each other, is often at the core of crime prevention and community policing strategies. Shanti Sena understand Rainbow Family values, needs, and communication idiosyncrasies and, hence, are better equipped than a non-Rainbow police force to use social pressure to gain compliance to their requests – which are usually reasonable and in accord with Rainbow Family values.

A key element in Rainbow peacekeeping strategies rests with the rules or norms the Shanti Sena seek to enforce. Put simply, they are minimally intrusive and reasonable – simple things like do not engage in commerce at the Gathering, do not drink alcohol, do not steal and do not fight. More important than the rules themselves is how they are adopted. In accordance with the anarchist principles that govern Gatherings, every Rainbow has an equal say in creating, defining and maintaining group norms and values. These are not laws imposed by a distant government but instead are a set of norms over which Gathering participants feel a sense of ownership and with the enforcement of which they have an inclination to cooperate. Hence, individuals have 'a deeper sense of the meaning and purpose' of the rules:

> The benefits of conceiving the social contract as an organic, ongoing agreement derived through direct participation and consensus decision making are manifold, not the least of which is to encourage an environment in which cooperation and not competition becomes the predominant aim of both the group and its individual constituents. (Amster, 2003, p. 19)

By enforcing a set of shared values crafted and adopted by popular consensus, Shanti Sena avoid the alienation and conflict associated with enforcing edicts that are at odds with community values. In the USA, such conflicts have historically poisoned community–police relations (Manning, 1988).

While Shanti Sena non-violence is tactically effective, the reasons for Shanti Sena adherence to non-violence are deeply rooted in Rainbow values. Any Rainbow Family sanctioning of violence would undermine their core commitment to promoting nonviolence. This absolute commitment to nonviolence runs contrary to the norm for policing in 'Babylon,' where, 'the sanctioning of violence in America grows from the mandate of the police to control social order at whatever cost' (Manning, 1980, p. 136). When police tactically surrender to violence, they legitimate violence and legitimate a society that accepts violence. Shanti Sena, in their 38-year adherence to tactical nonviolence, have avoided this slippery slope, allowing the Family to maintain a nonviolent ethos that is central to their communal identity.

Conflict with traditional police: a case study

While the Rainbow model of police-less policing has a strong track record for efficacy, it still baffles and frightens bureaucrats. For Babylonian police, the absence of traditionally recognizable law enforcement authorities, in and of itself, presents a threat to their notion of order. Governments apparently construe the nonviolent acephalous Gatherings as a great enough challenge to the legitimacy of rule by force, as to constitute a 'violent' attack that requires violent repression. This pattern is cross-culturally common (cf. Edo, Williams-Hunt, & Dentan, 2009). Apparently, just the existence of a Rainbow Gathering TAZ poses an existential threat to government control. A population's acquiescence to authority depends on its acceptance of the state's claim that only its monopoly of force can protect people from each other and guarantee their welfare. A peaceful TAZ undermines that claim while confronting law enforcement agencies with a vision of their own obsolescence. Without an authority structure they can recognize, governments tend to construe all such TAZs as violent (cf. Solnit, 2009). This violence is a 'factoid' in the original sense of the word: something which should be true if a cherished theory is correct and which therefore, adherents of that theory believe to be true, whatever the evidence (Niman, 2011, Epilogue 2).[7]

Today's US National Rainbow Gatherings draw a heavily armed paramilitary federal police force, arguably playing an unnecessary role, at a cost to taxpayers of, according to former US Forest Service Director of Law Enforcement John Twiss, approximately one million dollars per annual Gathering (Associated Press, 2008). Since late 1997, these expenditures fall under the province of a bureaucratic construct the Forest Service calls 'The National Incident Management Team' or 'NIMT' (NIMT, 2008, p. 4). The NIMT is based on the Forest Service Incident Command Team model, usually deployed in response to natural disasters such as forest fires, hurricanes, and volcanic eruptions. While their activities are mainly confined to the Gathering perimeter, where they establish vehicle inspection checkpoints, they also stage occasional incursions into the Gathering interior, usually looking for marijuana use or public nudity.[8] A 2008 American Civil Liberties Union (ACLU) investigation into US Forest Service treatment of the Rainbow Family at the 2008 National Gathering in Wyoming documented systematic abuses of the Rainbows not only at that Gathering, but determined that 'This type of harassment and general overzealous enforcement appear to have been the pattern in the USFS relationship with the Rainbow Family' (ACLU, 2008, p. 3).

The ACLU investigation stems from a 3 July 2008 NIMT assault on Kiddie Village, the Rainbow Family camp and kitchen for families with children – essentially the Family's day care center. Law enforcement officers (LEOs), in a 'speed-walking' pursuit of a person they suspected of sharing marijuana, followed their suspect into and subsequently shot up Kiddie Village with irritant-filled projectiles they identified as 'pepper balls.' The official USFS story, echoed nearly verbatim by the Associated Press (Neary, 2008), begins, 'About 400 members of the Rainbow Family threw rocks and sticks at ten federal officers on Thursday night as they tried to arrest one member of the group at its annual gathering in western Wyoming, the US Forest Service reported.' The article explains that the incident began when LEOs 'apprehended one person described as being uncooperative.' The arresting officers were then surrounded by a 'mob' of 'about 400 Rainbows' who 'began to advance, throwing sticks and rocks at the officers,' forcing the officers to employ 'crowd control tactics.'

Statements collected in a subsequent Department of Agriculture Office of Inspector General (OIG) 'Use of Force' investigation (OIG, 2009) provide more detail. One testimony begins with a '5–10 minute fast walking pursuit' of a man suspected 'of having marijuana.' This pursuit led to Kiddie Village, where the officer testified that he saw a woman 'move quickly past his security position' and interfere with the pursuit and arrest of the suspected marijuana smoker. Officers arrested the woman and were then reportedly surrounded by obscenity-shouting Rainbows. The LEOs drew their Tasers and 'aimed them at the ground.' The 'mob' reportedly advanced on the officers, causing them to discharge pepper ball weapons into the ground. 'Riotous' Rainbows supposedly pursued the LEOs and their prisoners through the woods for 30 minutes, pelting the officers with rocks. According to this testimony, Rainbows were 'running ahead through the forest, clearly in an attempt to outflank' officers in 'an aggressive action' (OIG, 2009, pp. 7–11).

Another officer testified that he 'deployed multiple pepper ball rounds to the chest and legs of subjects who were interfering or were assaultive, over the next 15–20 minutes,' adding 'These individuals in the riotous crowd displayed an advancing aggressive fighting stance, clenched fists, were tossing rocks, and made threatening statements to the officers …' A third officer testified to having drawn her Taser and pointed it at an individual who 'advanced' toward her (OIG, 2009, p. 11). A fourth LEO testified to shooting Rainbows 'who were not complying with the orders to get off the trail.' He 'only targeted non-compliant subjects and ensured he had a clear shot at his target prior to firing' (OIG, 2009, p. 12). Despite multiple LEO reports of Rainbows assaulting officers with sticks and stones during their half-mile 15–20 minute hike to exit the Gathering, no officers were injured (NIMT, 2008, p. 33).

The ACLU (2008, p. 1) interviewed veteran and 'casual' or 'first time' Gathering attendees, and 'Wyoming Residents that just wanted to see "what was going on."' Their 'reporters' included 'doctors, lawyers, National Guard members, a nurse, and a retired local carpenter.' The investigators also studied videos that Rainbow Family members shot using cell phones and small digital cameras, comparing video evidence to first-hand reports. They concluded that problems commenced with the arrest of a woman, who, as armed officers entered Kiddie Village, 'went up to one of the officers and asked a question.' The ACLU report states that 'there is no indication of what was said' in this exchange. 'This woman was then thrown to the ground, handcuffed and surrounded by several officers.' (p. 3) The ACLU concludes that 'at no time was it apparent that there were 400 individuals in the area' and 'at no time are there any rocks or sticks seen [by witnesses or on video] being thrown at the officers,' though 'one reporter states he may have seen 'one stick' thrown' (ACLU, 2008, p. 3).

Sequenced together, the LEO statements cited by the OIG investigation describe a chaotic police action with officers shouting contradictory commands, spraying aerosolized irritants and shooting people who they encountered on the trail as they exited the Gathering. As people moving down the trail in the opposite direction came close to this mobile melee, LEOs threatened to shoot them for approaching on the trail, shot them for remaining on the trail or identified them as a threat for leaving the trail and either 'running' through the forest in an 'aggressive' manner or moving through the woods in a 'stealthy' manner (OIG, 2009, pp. 10–12).[9] These confused officers escalated a routine marijuana arrest into an event where they caused the traumatization of innocent victims through their seemingly arbitrary use of weapons fire (cf. Kalafer, 2009). By contrast, the Rainbow Family Shanti Sena who responded to this incident appeared far better coordinated. They quickly formed a cordon separating the violent federal officers from the people in Kiddie Village and convinced them to clear a path for the officers to exit, while persuading young Rainbows to exercise restraint and not fight back against the LEOs. Some Shanti Sena peacekeepers performed this duty while federal LEOs shot them repeatedly in the back with pepper balls. A subsequently released internal Forest Service report indicates that officers were ready to employ 'deadly force' against Rainbows in Kiddie Village (NIMT, 2008, p. 11). Against this backdrop, the Rainbow Family's spontaneous Shanti Sena peacekeeping action may very well have saved lives on 3 July 2008.

Seasoned for violence

Relying on the same evidence, the ACLU investigation and the subsequent OIG investigation issued five months later appear at first glance to reach opposite conclusions. The ACLU condemned the Forest Service officers for abusing the Rainbows, while the government's internal OIG report exonerated their actions. At second glance, however, both reports are actually in line with each other, with the OIG report concluding, 'Investigation determined that actions taken by the FS LEOs, including their use of non-lethal force against the crowd, followed FS procedures, and were consistent with their training and FS policy' (OIG, 2009, p. 4). This is the problem (Niman, 2011, Epilogue Part 2).

Federal law enforcement agencies trained officers on duty at the Wyoming Gathering in a full complement of violent compliance techniques, including 'Striking and Close Quarter Defensive Tactics, Pressure Points, Weapon Retention, Takedowns, Ground Defense, Arrest Techniques, Baton Control Techniques, Edged Weapon Awareness, Oleoresin Capsicum Spray [and] Use of Force' (FLETC, 2009). The LEOs, however, appeared to lack training in nonviolent compliance techniques such as those the Shanti Sena applied to better effect during the event. There is also no evidence that the LEOs received any training in mediation or communication.

'The primary [Forest Service] objective for the 2008 National Rainbow Gathering was to provide a safe environment for officers and the participants, as well as, minimizing the environmental impacts from the event' (NIMT, 2008, p. 10). The Forest Service, in the wake of the Kiddie Village incident, removed all uniformed personnel from the Gathering, keeping them away for the next two days. Their absence successfully achieved their primary objective, articulated above, of making the Gathering safer for Rainbows and for themselves. This is evidenced by years of data showing that Rainbows have historically been abused primarily by LEOs (cf. Niman, 1997), and by LEO testimonies to the OIG documenting that they feel threatened and stressed while at the Gatherings. Witnesses to the Kiddie Village incident support this last fact, claiming to have seen terror in the eyes of the LEOs. Video evidence of the event also documents the fear level among officers. A review of internal government documents (Bridger Teton National Forest, 2008; NIMT, 2008, p. 11; Twiss, 2008; US Marshals Service, 2009, p. 3) indicates that both their training and their communication from superiors contained misleading information to induce fear of the Rainbows, despite their peaceful history and the centrality of nonviolence in their cultural identity (Amster, 2003, p. 17; Dentan, 1992, 1994; Niman, 1991, 1997; Solnit 2009, pp. 295–299).

This inordinate threat perception wears on the nerves of LEOs who work long shifts patrolling the culturally unfamiliar Gatherings.

Federal LEOs are often confused by nonviolent Rainbow Family responses to their heavy-handed tactics. In Babylon, police officers often disperse crowds by arresting or applying violence to random individuals, causing their cohort to scatter. While this tactic might prove effective with a riotous spring break crowd or after a sporting event, it has the opposite effect on Rainbows. Attack one, and many will stand in solidarity with the victim, albeit nonviolently. Civil rights activists employed this same strategy during the struggle against segregation, and Mahatma Gandhi's followers used it to defeat the British Empire. But to federal law enforcement officers at Rainbow Gatherings, the specter of a crowd circling or dropping to their knees in prayer, apparently fearless in the presence of weapons, adds to their terror (Niman, 2011, Epilogue Part 2).

In a similar vein, police stopped and ticketed two cyclists at the rear of a 2003 Critical Mass bike ride in Buffalo, NY. While the officers wrote traffic tickets, the remaining hundred-plus cyclists passed the hat and collected money for the two cyclists to pay their tickets, handing them the money as officers were still writing the tickets. Police responded by ticketing one of the donors for jaywalking. The remaining participants donated more money, causing the two officers to transmit an officer-in-distress call, apparently finding the riders' lack of fear as frightening. When more police arrived, they immediately arrested a rider. Rather than disperse, the other riders questioned the police about the arrest, causing the confused police to panic and violently attack the peaceful cyclists, who did not fight back (Jackson, 2003). As with the Rainbows, the police were incited not by violence, but by the absence of fear among members of the group, which in turn seemed to terrify them. As with the Rainbows, a much worse situation was averted by the cyclists' collective refrain from violent response. Being a temporary autonomous zone, like the Rainbow Gatherings, allowed the cyclists to scatter at the height of the violence and regroup a month later for a more tranquil ride.

Conclusion

Both Rainbow Shanti Sena and federal LEOs find their traditional tactics at their weakest at precisely the point where these two divergent cultures converge. Shanti Sena tactics are effective with Rainbows because Rainbow values support them, and, hence, Rainbows respect them. This support and respect bestow Shanti Sena with the social capital needed to easily gain compliance from Rainbows. The social forces that come into play when a disruptive Rainbow realizes that his or her actions mandate a Shanti Sena response, such as an Omming, often prove stronger than Babylon's weaponry. Forest Service LEOs, however, do not necessarily share Rainbow Family values and are not usually trained to understand or respect Shanti Sena or recognize and understand their nonviolent tactics. Hence, conflicts with Forest Service LEOs present the Shanti Sena model with its most difficult challenge. Ultimately, Shanti Sena are more successful in convincing Rainbows to maintain their nonviolence in the face of LEO threats and violence than they are in persuading the LEOs to cease their violence. Hence, during the Kiddie Village incident, Shanti Sena volunteers faced toward and communicated with the Rainbows, while being shot in the back by the LEOs.

Another major challenge to the Shanti Sena model is the inevitable manifestation of over-eager volunteers whose serial Shanti Sena actions make them appear as a sort of Rainbow Police agency. While Rainbows grapple with the periodic emergence of a nascent Shanti Sena 'force,' federal bureaucrats welcome and promote the idea of an organized Shanti Sena organization. Such an entity provides them with a collaboration partner they can understand and recognize, while undermining the democratic anarchy that so frightens them. Hence, Forest Service bureaucrats often seek out what they see as Shanti Sena representatives to negotiate with, instead of bringing their concerns before a democratic Rainbow Council.

Despite deep-seated values that preclude the formation of any sort of organized peacekeeping organization, Rainbows sometimes strategically play along with the bureaucrats, representing the Shanti Sena concept as a 'security force' when they believe that such a force is needed to appease Babylonian law enforcement officials. Internal Forest Service documents from the past 30 years evidence their promotion of 'a peacekeeping group or security team called Shantisena [*sic*]' who manage 'the internal peacekeeping at the Gathering site' (Colville National Forest Reports, 1981, cited in Niman, 1997, p. 121). Manifesting a Shanti Sena wizard has historically been to the Family's advantage, keeping Babylon's police generally at bay and outside of the Gatherings.

Providing an ersatz Shanti Sena organization to appease Babylonian police agencies, however, undermines the concept of a nonhierarchical spontaneous Shanti Sena, with the line between 'ersatz' and 'actual' dangerously blurred. Hence, Rainbows who volunteer for the task of interfacing with law enforcement agencies sometimes return into the Gathering acting more like confrontational police officers than like Shanti Sena. Rainbows respond to such tendencies by encouraging more active Shanti Sena participation from the general population, especially among groups, such as women, that are often underrepresented in traditional policing agencies. These diverse groups of fresh volunteers often overwhelm whatever authoritarian vibes the police-like Shanti Sena might put out. In a similar vein, councils often recruit and dispatch new Shanti Sena volunteers bringing music, food and love to hotspots such as A-Camp (cf. Grant, 2003, p. 230; Niman, 1997, p. 123).

Not all conflicts, and especially those with government authorities, can be harmonized by Shanti Sena actions. In those cases, conflict is not necessarily resolved but averted or escaped as the Rainbows dissolve their TAZ at the conclusion of each Gathering and disperse into Babylon, only to reappear with essentially the same city in another time and place. Where revolutionaries aim to control territory, the TAZ avoids prolonged conflict with the state and instead 'liberates an area (of land, of time, of imagination) and then dissolves itself to reform elsewhere' (Bey, 1991, pp. 100–101). A utopian experiment can persist through the regular movement of 'the entire tribe' (p. 102). To police authorities, the apparent retreat of the Rainbows might appear as surrender, which would satisfy their quest to control or dominate the Family. Or at the very least, police agencies might view their problem as over, since the Rainbows are gone, albeit to another time or place. Demographers refer to this practice as a 'fission–fusion' (cf. Dentan, 1992, 1994, 2008, p. 116; Fix, 1975; Neel, Salzano, Junquerira, Keiter, & Maybury Lewis, 1964). For the Rainbows, it is at the core of a nonviolent survival strategy that has allowed the Family to persist for 38 years while spreading itself and its Shanti Sena peacekeeping model around the globe.

Notes

1. Rainbows borrow the term 'Babylon' from the Rastafarian movement, who in turn gleaned the term from the Book of Revelation.
2. US National Gatherings officially last a week, but with set-up and clean-up can stretch out over a two-month period.

3. Kropotkin claims such 'liberty worked a miracle. The insane became cured. Even those who had incurable lesions became sweet, tractable members of the family.' Like a Rainbow Gathering, Gheel offered its guests full membership in a nurturing supportive community. The Gheel experiment ended in 1856 with the construction of a more typical infirmary, after the murder of the village's Burgomaster (A report on the care of the insane poor: II. Old Gheel, 1905).
4. Critical Mass is an acephalous movement of bicyclists that gather, usually at a predetermined monthly time, for a mass ride that swells to fill thoroughfares, usually crowding out automotive traffic and liberating a safe car-free space for cycling.
5. Rainbows use Om circles not only for peacekeeping, but also for opening meetings and councils, and in preparation to eat a communal meal.
6. This is one of the most important mantras in Tantric Buddhism (e.g. Evans-Wentz, 1960, 1967, pp. 127, 301, 312, 320–322, 340), believed to open the user's mind to a higher dimension (Kapleau, 1966, p. 346).
7. In the case of the Rainbow Gatherings, this evidence is overwhelming. This non-force of instantaneous Shanti Sena has a strong 38-year track record for peacekeeping – as evidenced both in media reports and nearly four decades worth of US Forest Service reports documenting and statistically summarizing activity at the Gatherings, many of which were released to this author in compliance with the federal Freedom of Information Act (FOIA). Such recently released documents are available for download at an archive hosted by Buffalo State College in New York (http://buffalostate.edu/peopleoftherainbow).
8. Usually found in swimming and washing areas.
9. Video evidence also documents witness allegations of LEOs pointing Taser weapons at the faces of Rainbow Family members.

References

ACLU. (2008). *Rainbow Family Gathering in Wyoming.* Retrieved January 18, 2010, from www.aclu-wy.org/NewsEvents/PressReleases/10_8_08.pdf

Amster, R. (2003). Restoring (dis)order: Sanctions, resolutions, and 'social control' in anarchist communities. *Contemporary Justice Review, 6*(1), 9–24.

A report on the care of the insane poor: II. Old Gheel. (1905). *British Medical Journal, 1*(2298), 96.

Associated Press. (2008, October 4). Report says Forest Service has harassed Gatherings. *New York Times.* Retrieved January 7, 2010, from www.nytimes.com/2008/10/05/us/05rainbow.html

Bey, H. (1991). *T.A.Z.: The temporary autonomous zone, ontological anarchy, poetic terrorism.* Brooklyn, NY: Autonomedia.

Bridger Teton National Forest. (2008, June 26). *Safety and health reminders.* Retrieved January 20, 2010, from www.buffalostate.edu/peopleoftherainbow/x519.xml

Carlsson, C. (2002). *Critical Mass: Bicycling's defiant celebration.* Oakland, CA: AK Press.

Dentan, R.K. (1992). The rise, maintenance and destruction of peaceable polity; a preliminary essay in political ecology. In J. Silverberg & J.P. Gray (Eds.), *Aggression and peacefulness in humans and other primates* (pp. 214–257). New York: Oxford University Press.

Dentan, R.K. (1994). 'Surrendered men': Peaceable enclaves in the post-enlightenment West. In L. Sponsel & T. Gregor (Eds.), *The anthropology of peace and nonviolence* (pp. 69–108). Boulder, CO: Lynne Rienner.

Dentan, R.K. (2008). *Overwhelming terror: Love, fear, peace, and violence among Semai of Malaysia.* Lanham, MD: Rowman & Littlefield.

Edo, J., Williams-Hunt, A., & Dentan, R.K. (2009). 'Surrender,' peacekeeping, and internal colonialism: A neglected episode in Malaysian history. *Bijdragen tot de Taal, Land en Volkenkunde, 165*(2–3), 216–240.

Evans-Wentz, W.Y., ed. (1960). *The Tibetan book of the dead or the after-death experiences on the Bardo Olance, according to Lama Kazi Dawa – Samdup's English rendering* (2nd. ed.). Oxford: Oxford University Press.

Evans-Wentz, W.Y. (1967). *Tibetan yoga and secret doctrines or seven books of wisdom of the great path, according to the late Lama Kazi Dawa – Sandup's English rendering.* Oxford: Oxford University Press.

Fix, A.G. (1975). Fission–fusion and lineal effect: Aspects of the population structure of the Semai Senoi of Malaysia. *American Journal of Physical Anthropology, 43*, 295–302.

FLETC (Federal Law Enforcement Training Center). (2009). *Law Enforcement Control Tactics Refresher Training Program.* Retrieved January 9, 2010, from www.fletc.gov/training/programs

Grant, R. (2003). *American nomads: Travels with lost conquistadors, mountain men, cowboys, Indians, hoboes, truckers, and bull riders.* New York: Grove Press.

Jackson, B. (2003, June 25). Buffalo cops wage war on pedal pushers: Iatrogenic law enforcement on the Niagara frontier. *Counterpunch.* Retrieved May 30, 2010, from www.counterpunch.org

Kalafer, J. (2009). *We love you* [DVD]. Mendham, NJ: New Jersey Pictures.

Kapleau, P. (1966). Notes on Zen vocabulary and Buddhist doctrine. In P. Kapleau (Ed. and Trans.), *The three pillars of Zen: Teaching, practice, and enlightenment* (pp. 321–350). New York: Harper & Row.

Kropotkin, P. (2002[1877]). Prisons and their moral influence on prisoners. In R.N. Baldwin (Ed.), *Anarchism: A collection of revolutionary writings* (pp. 230–235). Mineola, NY: Dover.

Manning, P. (1980). Violence and the police role. *Annals of the American Academy of Political and Social Science, 452*, 135–144.

Manning, P. (1988). Community policing as a drama of control. In J. Greene & S. Mastrofski (Eds.), *Community policing: Rhetoric or reality* (pp. 27–45). New York: Praeger.

McClusky, L. (2003, October 17–18). *The meaning of bicycle culture's anarchist rebellion.* Paper presented at the 51st annual meetings of the New York State Sociological Association, Loudonville, NY.

McClusky, L. (2004, February 19–22). *Why critical mass? Understanding bicycle activism.* Paper presented at the 74th annual meeting of the Eastern Sociological Society, New York.

Neary, B. (2008, July 7). *Official: Rainbow incident could have been worse.* New York: Associated Press.

Neel, J.V., Salzano, F.M., Junquerira, P.C., Keiter, F., & Maybury Lewis, D. (1964). Studies on the Xavante Indians of the Brazilian Mato Grosso. *American Journal of Human Genetics, 16*, 52–140.

Niman, M.I. (1991). *The Rainbow Family: An ethnography from within* (PhD dissertation, University at Buffalo, Buffalo, NY).

Niman, M.I. (1997). *People of the Rainbow: A nomadic utopia.* Knoxville, TN: University of Tennessee Press.

Niman, M.I. (2011) *People of the Rainbow: A nomadic utopia, volume 2.* Knoxville, TN: University of Tennessee Press.

NIMT. (2008, July 7). *Incident summary.* Retrieved January 20, 2010, from http://www.buffalostate.edu/peopleoftherainbow/documents/WY-08-NIMT.pdf

OIG (US Department of Agriculture Office of Inspector General). (2009, February 27). *Use of force report* (pp. 3–113). Retrieved accessed January 20, 2010, from http://www.buffalostate.edu/peopleoftherainbow/documents/FOIA-Dec09-OIG.pdf

Pepinsky, H. (2000). Cultivating community in conversational circles. *Contemporary Justice Review, 3*(2), 175–186.

Solnit, R. (2009). *A paradise built in hell: The extraordinary communities that arise in disaster.* New York: Viking.

Twiss, J.C. (2008, July 21). *Letter.* Retrieved January 20, 2010, from www.buffalostate.edu/peopleoftherainbow/x520.xml.

US Marshals Service. (2009). *Operational plan.* Retrieved January 20, 2010, from http://www.buffalostate.edu/peopleoftherainbow/documents/MS-09-OpPLan.pdf

Civilian oversight as a public good: democratic policing, civilian oversight, and the social

Danielle Hryniewicz

Department of Sociology, University of Western Ontario, London, ON N6A 5C2, Canada

In recent years, a number of community groups have mounted public campaigns for civilian oversight of police complaint processes, as 'police investigating police' is seen as failing to adhere to a principle of democratic policing: police are accountable to civilian authority. Drawing on notions of policing as a public good, I argue that civilian oversight is a source of physical and ontological security. In developing this perspective, I offer an explanation as to why policing scholars and persons affiliated with community groups might advocate for the use of civilian oversight, and consider a model by which to enhance perceptions of public security.

> Democratic policing supplies a small but vital component of the resources of secure belonging. (Loader, 2006, p. 210)

In recent years, a number of community groups have mounted public campaigns for civilian oversight of police complaint processes, as the act of 'police investigating police' is seen to violate a fundamental principle of democratic policing: police are accountable to civilian authority and the needs of *all* civilians (Goldsmith & Lewis, 2000; Landau, 1996; LeSage, 2005; Lewis, 1999; Lewis & Prenzler, 1999). Consequently, police abuses of authority reinforce the notion that some degree of civilian control of state agencies is necessary for the legitimacy of democratic states (Herbert, 2006). To this end, civilian oversight bodies are thought to generate a climate of accountability, openness and transparency in the communities they serve (Walker, 2005).

Thus far, discussions of civilian oversight have largely centred on issues of police accountability and legitimacy. The ways in which civilian oversight may contribute to the reaffirmation of 'community', 'citizenship' and 'public security', however, have been less often considered within the policing literature. In this article, I critically reflect upon the political significance of 'civilian oversight'. My aim is to expand existing claims as to why we need external review and more specifically civilian oversight. With reference to Loader's (1997a, 1997b, 1999, 2000, 2006, 2007; Loader & Walker, 2001) work, I argue that civilian oversight, as a form of external review, is consistent with the principles of democratic policing. Contrary to internal forms of review, civilian oversight is seemingly generative of community support for public police. Hence, a more critical analysis of civilian oversight reveals an increasingly complex picture: civilian oversight is a source of physical and ontological security. In exploring this claim, I answer the following question with reference to Loader and Walker's (2001) notion of policing as a public good: How does the idea of public security help us to justify our need for civilian oversight of police complaint processes?

In developing and illustrating this perspective, I also offer an explanation as to why policing scholars and persons affiliated with community organizations advocate for the use of civilian oversight. In the pages that follow, I provide a literature review of civilian oversight and its political relevance to democratic policing. Second, I discuss the ways in which civilian oversight is a source of public security and, by extension, a public good. Finally, I consider a strategy by which to enhance perceptions of public security in relation to civilian oversight.

Why is civilian oversight politically significant?

> … The task is to engage citizens in public dialogue about policing in ways that enable them to see that the security and political freedom of each and all is more likely to be nurtured and protected through their participation with others in forms of common deliberation. (Loader, 2006, p. 281)

Public policing efforts rely on and involve a diverse array of community agencies and organizations. Persons working within community agencies assume a pivotal role in public policing by overseeing the social control efforts of the police and other state agencies. For instance, agency staff might assist in Restorative Justice[1] programmes through which the offender, victim and staff work together to repair and rebuild the fractured community bonds.

Community representatives may also participate in civilian review processes to evaluate potential cases of police misconduct and corruption. Representatives are thought to be objective, impartial judges, who advocate for their civilian constituencies. A respondent in Beattie and Weitzer's (2000) study captures this sentiment: 'I hope the review board is made up of people who are able to look at the situation in an unbiased fashion. Civilians view the situations differently than the police do, and we need someone to represent the opinion of civilians' (p. 42). The presence of civilians within police complaint processes is said to enhance police credibility, accountability, and ultimately, public confidence in police services (Watt, 1991).

Given the importance of the citizens' role in policing projects, the police must understand themselves as subservient to the community, and allow for citizens to evaluate police performance and assist in the construction of police policy (Herbert, 2006). Without such responsiveness, 'the police's inquest for legitimacy might well suffer' (Herbert, 2006, p. 69; see also Huey, 2007).

Sustaining legitimacy is a central leadership obligation (Manning, 2001). The police must cultivate '… the inchoate, supportive feelings towards policing that exist within society' (Loader 1997a, p. 5) and capitalize on pre-existing symbolic capital between police and nation. A failure to do so may inhibit the development of effective community–police partnerships (Goldsmith & Lewis, 2000). Previous research has revealed that the lack of transparency evident within the internal handling of police complaints can be a significant barrier to police legitimacy, accountability and, in turn, to community support for public police (Hryniewicz, 2008; Landau, 2000).

Police accountability, a concept central to the discussion of community support for public police, encompasses issues of poverty, racism, homelessness and, in turn, the social movements that address these issues (Ceric, 2001). In Canada, the limitations of traditional, internal complaint processes have been documented by the Aboriginal Legal Services of Toronto (ALST). According to the ALST, '... there is sufficient, in fact substantial, empirical evidence, to show that communities do not have confidence in an oversight body that is not independent of the police, nor accessible to each community member ... The entire police complaints process lacks credibility in the Aboriginal community' (2003, p. 1).

PIVOT Legal Society in Vancouver has reported similar findings. According to PIVOT (2004), marginalized citizens (e.g. homeless persons) who are the victims of police misconduct do not often trust the police to complete a fair investigation. Furthermore, marginalized victims fear retaliation by police officers if they do make a complaint (PIVOT, 2004).

In addressing the limitations of traditional complaint processes, civilian oversight seeks to deepen and extend expressions of citizenship – among all citizens – by presenting itself as an ongoing collective project in community policing (PIVOT, 2004). Citizens, united by a common need for security, derive an identity and sense of *security* from their attachment to a political community (Loader, 2006).

In this context, 'security' refers to the risks and dangers inherent in and a product of the environment. 'Security' encompasses the resources individuals and groups use to manage the unease that is generated by the risk of victimization (Loader, 2006). For instance, the police perform a security management function in which they are involved in restricting the exposure of members of the public to an array of physical and ontological dangers.

In reviewing the policing literature on civilian oversight, one theme persists: civilian oversight is inextricably linked to discussions of police accountability and legitimacy. In what follows, I consider the role of civilian oversight within public policing and democratic governance.

Civilian oversight as a public good

> Our sense of safety and security is irreducibly social and deeply implicated in our relationship with others. (Loader & Walker, 2001, p. 26)

In exploring the associations between democratic policing, civilian oversight and the 'social', one must consider an often-overlooked aspect of public policing: the contribution of democratic policing to the social lies in task performance (Loader, 2006). Policing tasks must be performed in ways that sustain the conditions of a democratic 'common life' in which the security of all individuals and groups is protected (Loader, 2006). To this end, civilian oversight provides a way in which the police may reinforce and rationalize their public function as 'democratic protectors'.

Public participation within the review process is fundamental to democratic governance and societal order. The external investigation of police complaints provides citizens with a mechanism by which they can reaffirm their social values; citizens are able to critically question and influence state proceedings. Hence, the contribution that civilian oversight makes to security provides citizens with a 'token' (Loader, 2006, p. 214) of their membership to a political community. Members of marginalized communities, such as the homeless, the disabled and the Aboriginal community, share a vested interest with members of non-marginalized communities to ensure that police efforts and actions are legitimate. It follows, then, that individuals who advocate for external review are defending something that is inherently social: a desire for common security and protection from undemocratic acts.

Civilian oversight provides a political platform that all citizens, in theory, can access. Through civilian oversight, citizens engage the state in public dialogue, raising concerns that are responded to and considered within policy forums. As Loader (2006) contends, public dialogue is fundamental to political processes, as it demonstrates an important truth: the security and political freedom of each person is more likely to be nurtured and protected through their participation with others. In other words, the securities and freedoms of one are inextricably linked to those of another. Our physical safety and ontological sense of security are irreducibly social and deeply implicated in our relationship with others (Loader & Walker, 2001).

In considering civilian oversight as a source of public security, we might further this statement and make the claim that civilian oversight is a primary and fundamental example of a 'public good'; a good that is a prerequisite to the generation of other political goods (Loader & Walker, 2001). 'Public goods' are thought to be implicated in the process through which justice and equality are conceived (Loader & Walker, 2001). In the present case, civilian oversight serves as the catalyst by which democratic principles are reinforced and readapted. During the external review process, civilians and police personnel collaborate and consider political issues. Ultimately, both police and non-police persons work together to re-instil public safety and confidence in the police.

If we consider civilian oversight as a constitutive public good – a 'source of security whose actualization is so pivotal to the purpose of community that it helps to construct and sustain our "we-feeling" and our very sense of "common publicness"' (Loader & Walker, 2007, p. 164) – we must consider the political implications of this claim. We must ask ourselves how the processes of civilian oversight enhance public security.

Civilian oversight: a security-enhancing strategy

> There is a tendency for the quality of security to be enhanced in the case of any particular individual when the security of those with whom that individual shares a social environment is also reasonably attended to. (Loader & Walker, 2007, p. 161)

As observed by Loader (2000), policing commissions are intended to fulfil their remit in ways that sustain considerations of democratic deliberation, equity and effectiveness in the delivery of policing and security services. In light of Loader's (2000) discussion of plural policing and democratic governance, I consider four *critical* dimensions of the civilian review process: public agreement, democratic decision-making, public accountability and evaluation.

Public agreement

Quite simply, civilian review boards aim to arrive at decisions that secure the broadest levels of public agreement without either: '... (1) prejudicing the active rights of any individual or social group affected by the decision; or (2) acting in ways that are disproportionately detrimental to the other interests and aspirations of such individuals and groups' (Loader, 2000, p. 338). From this perspective, the unwarranted 'over-' (or overly invasive) policing of particular individuals, as well as the 'under-policing' and inability of marginalized civilians to acquire a proportionate level of policing resources, are considered undemocratic and thus unacceptable actions.

Democratic decision-making

Civilian review boards are responsible for arriving at decisions that are democratically constituted. A variety of agencies, which are publicly funded and 'democratically steered' (Loader, 2000, p. 339), assist in the review and are provided with an opportunity to select community representatives who actively participate in the review proceedings.

Public accountability

The rationale underpinning this dimension is to '... enable an unbroken chain of legitimation to be traced from any one of the plethora of agencies who may be undertaking (governmental) policing functions to some form of democratically constituted political authority' (Loader, 2000, p. 339). In other words, the agencies and community groups participating in the review processes are accountable to the public. As in the case of police institutions, citizens participating in the review process are must consider and uphold the principles of democratic governance central to police operations. Public support for civilian review processes hinges on positive perceptions of the police (non-civilian) and community (civilian) organizations.

Evaluation

Evaluation provides a vital addition to the review committees' functions. Citizens are able to '... reflexively supervise the delivery of [complaint] processes across a locality and remove or replace agencies whose performance serves to undermine the considerations of equity, effectiveness and democracy that the commission has been constituted to protect' (Loader, 2000, p. 340).

Discussion

Meaningful civilian involvement in the handling of public complaints against the police has been a focus of scholars, police reformers and commissions of inquiry for some time. Intermittent scandals involving police mistreatment of ethnic minority individuals and groups have contributed to recent calls for reform in the Canadian context and elsewhere (PIVOT, 2004).

In response to these and other incidents, a number of community groups have mounted campaigns for civilian oversight of police complaint processes. Incidents of police misconduct reinforce the notion that some degree of civilian control of state agencies is necessary for the legitimacy of democratic states (Herbert, 2006). Civilian oversight bodies are thought to generate accountability, openness and transparency in the communities they serve (Walker, 2005).

I have argued that civilian oversight of policing is a source of both physical and ontological security. Civilian oversight expresses and gives effect to an idea of a society that is an ongoing, collective project, enabling citizens to derive an identity and sense of security from their membership of, and attachment to, a political community.

As a source of security, civilian oversight is a vehicle by which democratic principles are reinforced and readapted. Individuals who advocate for external review are defending something that is inherently social: a desire for common security and protection from undemocratic acts. Given that civilian oversight is linked to notions of citizenship, community and security, it is imperative that future research evaluates the extent to which individuals and community organizations feel confidence in their local police complaint process. In soliciting the views of marginalized citizens (who are often excluded from civilian review processes), we will gain insight as to how police governing agencies (i.e. police review boards and civilian oversight committees) can best assist in the fostering of civic solidarity and identification across the boundaries of local or ethnic community.

Note

1. An approach to justice where offenders are encouraged to take responsibility for their actions and to repair the harm they have done by apologizing, returning stolen money or doing community service.

References

Aboriginal Legal Services of Toronto. (2003). *Race relations draft report.* Retrieved July 10, 2009, from http://aboriginallegal.ca/docs/JWG.htm

Beattie, C., & Weitzer, R. (2000). Race, democracy and law: Civilian review in Washington, DC. In A. Goldsmith & C. Lewis (Eds.), *Civilian oversight of policing: Governance, democracy and human rights* (pp. 63–79). Oxford: Hart Publishing.

Ceric, I. (2001). Organizing accountability: Community legal clinics and police complaints. *Journal of Law & Social Policy, 16*, 241–260.

Goldsmith, A., & Lewis, C. (2000). *Civilian oversight of policing.* Oxford: Hart Publishing.

Herbert, S. (2006). *Civilians, cops, and power: Recognizing the limits of community.* Chicago, IL: University of Chicago.

Huey, L. (2007). *Negotiating demands: The politics of skid row policing in Edinburgh, San Francisco and Vancouver.* Toronto: University of Toronto Press.

Hryniewicz, D. (2008). *Conflict Mediation Services of Downsview: Restorative justice program – Service evaluation and review 2006 cases.* Toronto: Conflict Mediation Services of Downsview.

Landau, T. (1996). When police investigate police: A view from complainants. *Canadian Journal of Criminology, 38*(3), 291–315.

Landau, T. (2000). Back to the future: The death of civilian review of public complaints against the police in Ontario, Canada. In A. Goldsmith & C. Lewis (Eds.), *Civilian oversight of policing: Governance, democracy and human rights* (pp. 63–79). Oxford: Hart Publishing.

LeSage, P.J. (2005). *Report on the police complaints system in Ontario.* Toronto: Gowlings.

Lewis, C. (1999). *Complaints against police: The politics of reform.* Sydney: Hawkins Press.

Lewis, C., & Prenzler, T. (1999). Civilian oversight of police in Australia. *Trends and Issues in Crime and Criminal Justice, 141*, 1–6.

Loader, I. (1997a). Policing and the social: Questions of symbolic power. *British Journal of Sociology, 48*(1), 1–18.

Loader, I. (1997b). Thinking normatively about private security. *Journal of Law and Society, 24*(3), 377–394.

Loader, I. (1999). Consumer culture and the commodification of policing and security. *Sociology, 33*(2), 373–392.

Loader, I. (2000). Plural policing and democratic governance. *Social and Legal Studies, 9*(3), 323–345.

Loader, I. (2006). Policing, recognition, and belonging. *ANNALS of the American Academy of Political and Social Science, 605*, 201–221.

Loader, I., & Walker, N. (2001). Policing as a public good: Reconstituting the connections between policing and the state. *Theoretical Criminology, 5*(1), 9–35.

Loader, I., & Walker, N. (2007). *Civilizing security.* London: Cambridge University Press.

Manning, P.K. (2001). Theorizing policing: The drama and myth of crime control in the NYPD. *Theoretical Criminology, 5*(3), 315–344.

PIVOT. (2004). *Towards more effective police oversight.* Retrieved from http://www.pivotlegal.org/pdfs/Effective_Police_Oversight-Sept2004.pdf

Walker, S. (2005). *What real police accountability looks like: The '120 shots' incident and the Los Angeles Sheriff's Department Response.* Omaha, NE: Police Professionalism Initiative, University of Nebraska.

Watt, S. (1991). The future of civilian oversight of policing. *Canadian Journal of Criminology, 3*(33), 347–362.

Where abolition meets action: women organizing against gender violence

Vikki Law

Independent Researcher

The last decade has seen a growing movement toward abolishing prisons. At the same time, antiviolence organizers have called on prison abolitionists to take the issue of gender violence seriously and to develop initiatives to address it in the context of prison abolition. Fueled by increasing recognition that women of color, immigrant, queer, transgender, poor, and other marginalized women are often further brutalized – rather than protected – by the police, grassroots groups, and activists throughout the world, are organizing community alternatives to calling 911. Such initiatives, however, are not new. Throughout history, women have acted and organized to ensure their own and their loved ones' safety. This article examines both past and present models of women's community self-defense practices against interpersonal violence. By exploring methods women have employed to protect themselves, their loved ones, and communities, this article seeks to contribute to the current conversations on how to promote safety and accountability without resorting to state-based policing and prisons.

During the last decade, the growing movement toward prison abolition, coupled with mounting recognition of the need for community responses to gender violence, has led to increased interest in developing alternatives to government policing. Moving away from the notion of women as victims in need of police protection, grassroots groups, and activists are organizing community alternatives to calling 911. Such initiatives, however, are not new. Throughout the twentieth century, women have organized alternative models of self-protection.

This piece examines past and present models of women's community self-defense practices against violence. By exploring the wide-ranging methods women across the globe have employed to protect themselves, their loved ones, and communities, this piece seeks to contribute to current conversations on promoting safety and accountability without resorting to state-based policing and prisons.

Storytelling to connect past, present, and future

Connecting past efforts to current initiatives allows us to both envision a future in which police and prisons are not the sole solutions to gender violence and to know that such possibilities can – and, in some small pockets, do or did – exist.

In 2004, Mimi Kim launched Creative Interventions, a resource center to promote community-based responses to interpersonal violence. Recognizing that, while activists and others are increasingly embracing the idea of community-based accountability as an alternative to the police, many have difficulty envisioning what accountability processes might look like. The group developed STOP (StoryTelling and Organizing Project), a resource for people to share their experiences with community-based accountability models and interventions to domestic violence, family violence, and sexual abuse. 'In a lot of ways, we are building a long, long history of everyday people trying to end violence in ways that don't play into oppressive structures,' she stated (Huang, 2008, p. 60).

In their 2001 statement on gender violence and incarceration, Critical Resistance and INCITE! Women of Color Against Violence challenged communities to not only come up with ways to creatively address violence, but also to document these processes: 'Transformative practices emerging from local communities should be documented and disseminated to promote collective responses to violence' (Critical Resistance and INCITE! 2001). By connecting past and current organizing initiatives from across the globe, 'Where Abolition Meets Actions' hopes to contribute to the conversations around safety and abolition as well as inspires readers to organize in their own communities.

The 1970s (women's liberation: defending themselves and each other)

Women's liberation movements of the 1970s allowed women to begin talking openly about their experiences of sexual assault. Discussions led to a growing realization that women need to take their safety into their own hands and fight back.

Some women formed street patrols to watch for and prevent violence against women. In Cambridgeport, Massachusetts, members of Women's Liberation group Cell 16 began patrolling the streets where women often left their factory jobs after dark. 'We were studying Tae Kwan Do and decided to intentionally patrol, offering to accompany women to their cars or to public transportation,' recalled former Cell 16 member Roxanne Dunbar-Ortiz. 'The first time two of us went to the nearby factory to offer our services to women workers, the first woman we approached looked terrified and hurried away. We surmised that my combat boots and army surplus garb were intimidating, so after that I dressed more conventionally.'

Later efforts were better received: Dunbar-Ortiz recalled that one night Cell 16 members met Mary Ann Weathers, an African-American woman, at a film screening. 'After the film we introduced ourselves and told her we provided escorts for women. We asked her if she would like us to walk her home, as it was near midnight. Mary Ann Weathers, who joined our group, marveled over the bizarre and wonderful experience of having five white women volunteer to protect her' (Dunbar-Ortiz, 2001, p. 136).

Dunbar-Ortiz also recalled that she traveled around the country speaking and encouraging women to form similar patrols. Students at Iowa State University and the University of Kentucky responded, forming patrols on their campus.

The lack of police and judicial response to gender violence led to increasing recognition that women needed to learn to physically defend themselves from male violence.

In 1969, Cell 16 established Tae Kwan Do classes for women. Unlike existing police offered self-defense classes that promoted fear rather than empowerment, Cell

16's classes challenged students to draw the connections between their learned sense of helplessness and their role in society as women (Lafferty & Clark, 1970, pp. 96–97).

In 1974, believing that all people had the right to live free from violence and recognizing that women were often disproportionately impacted by violence, Nadia Telsey and Annie Ellman started Brooklyn Women's Martial Arts (BWMA) in New York City. 'I have felt that it [self-defense] is connected to self-determination,' stated Ellman. 'We wanted to take our training into our own hands to prevent and avoid violence. We developed programs to reflect and understand that many people who came to our program were oppressed not just because they were women; there were multiple oppressions going on and we felt it was important to address them all.'

By the mid-1970s, the concept of women's self-defense had become so popular that the demand for training sometimes exceeded the number of available instructors. A 1975 issue of *Black Belt Woman*, a feminist martial arts publication, ran an ad for certified women teachers by the Meechee Dojo in Minneapolis to fill the daily requests for self-defense workshops by schools, community groups, and continuing education programs (Lehmann, 1975, p. 19).

The idea of women taking training into their own hands to protect them from violence did not dissolve after the 1970s. Some of the programs and schools founded in the 1970s, such as the BWMA (renamed the Center for Anti-Violence Education or CAE in 1989) and Feminists in Self-Defense Training (FIST) in Olympia, Washington, continue teaching women's self-defense today. Women's groups that emerged in later decades also took on the task of teaching women to defend themselves. In 1992, women in Taos, New Mexico, responded to police indifference to gender violence by forming the Taos Women's Self-Defense Project. Within two years, the Project had taught self-defense to over 400 women, presenting classes in public schools, businesses and health departments (Giggans, 1994, p. 41).

Although much of the 1970s rhetoric and organizing around gender violence presupposed that women were attacked by strangers, women also recognized and organized against violence perpetrated by those that they know, including spouses and intimate partners. In Neu-Isenburg, a small town near Frankfurt, Germany, a group of women called Fan-Shen decided that, rather than establish a shelter for battered women, they would force the abuser out of the house. When a battered woman called the local women's shelter, the group arrived at her home to not only confront her abuser, but also occupy the house as round-the-clock guards to the woman until her abuser moved out. When the strategy was reported in 1977, Fan-Shen had already been successful in five instances ('Women's Patrol,' 1977, p. 18).

Anti-violence organizing in communities of color

Women's Liberation groups were not the only ones to recognize the need for alternative models of preventing gender violence. Communities of color in the USA also developed methods to ensure women's safety without relying on a system that has historically ignored their safety or further threatened it by using gender violence as a pretext for increased force, brutality, and mass incarceration against community members.

In 1979, when Black women were found brutally murdered in Boston's primarily Black Roxbury and Dorchester neighborhoods, residents organized the Dorchester Green Light Program. The program provided identifiable safe houses for women who were threatened or assaulted on the streets. Program coordinators, who lived in

Dorchester, visited and spoke at community groups and gatherings in their areas. Residents interested in opening their homes as safe houses filled out applications, which included references and descriptions of the house living situation. The program screened each application and checked the references. Once accepted, the resident attended orientation sessions, which included self-defense instruction. They were then given a green light bulb for their porch light; when someone was at home, the green light was turned on as a signal to anyone in trouble. Within eight months, over 100 safe houses had been established (Dejanikus & Kelly, 1979, p. 7).

At a 1986 conference on ending violence against women at UCLA, Beth Richie spoke about a community-based intervention program in East Harlem, a New York neighborhood that was predominantly Black and Latino. Community residents organized to take responsibility for women's safety. 'Safety watchers' visited the house when called by the abused person or the neighbors. They encouraged the abuser to leave; if the abuser refused, the watchers stayed in the house. Their presence prevented further violence, at least while they were present. 'Beth feels violence will probably continue but community consciousness has been raised,' noted one conference attendee. 'In these communities, people do not call the police fearing more violence from the police. Men are not going to jail because the communities are working together' (Bustamante, 1986, p. 14).

Precedents and influences

Women's collective action and organizing to protect themselves and each other did not originate in the 1970s. In fact, some of the methods that emerged during the 1970s had been utilized by women's groups of the past.

In the 1920s, as more women began working in Shanghai's cotton mills, they formed *jiemei hui* or sisterhood societies. In addition to providing acceptable ways for women to spend time together in a gender-segregated society, the *jiemei hui* also offered protection to their members. Local hoodlums gathered at the mill gates and seized women's wages on paydays; on ordinary days, they collected money by 'stripping a sheep' (robbing a woman of her clothes and selling them for money). Female gangsters specialized in the lucrative business of kidnapping young girls to sell to brothels or as future daughters-in-law. Sexual abuse was a pervasive threat: many workers had family members or friends who had been raped, beaten, or kidnapped by neighborhood hoodlums. Members of sisterhoods walked together to and from the mills to protect each other from harassment and attacks. The number of *jiemei hui* increased during the Japanese occupation of Shanghai when women faced the additional threat of assault by Japanese soldiers (Honig, 1997, p. 490).

During the same period, another form of women's communal self-defense emerged in rural China. During the uneasy alliance between the Kuomintang (Nationalist Party) and the Communists during the 1920s, women propagandists organized Women's Associations in rural villages to provide support for the armies. Village women, however, began mobilizing around their immediate concerns such as foot binding, women's education, a woman's right to divorce, and abuse. Women's Associations assumed the right to punish abusive husbands and in-laws, often through public humiliation (Croll, 1978, p. 202). In Hankou and other areas, the Women's Associations forced the offending spouse or in-law to walk through the streets wearing a dunce cap and shouting slogans on behalf of women's freedom (Strong, 1928, p. 126).

The 1927 split between the Kuomintang and the Communists halted the burgeoning women's movement. The Kuomintang suppressed Women's Associations, arresting, punishing, and even executing known members. During the Japanese invasion, however, women propagandists once again followed the Communist armies to rural villages and instigated the formation of new Women's Associations.

Unlike their predecessors, Communist propagandists were met with skepticism about the possibility of ending abuse and gaining social and economic equality. The breakthrough came with the 'speak bitterness' meetings in which women were encouraged to talk about their sufferings. While propagandists originally encouraged women to hold these meetings against their local landlords, many identified their husbands and in-laws as their immediate oppressors. In these meetings, each woman learned that many other women in her village experienced the same oppressions. These women, who had been raised with the ancient notion that women were inferior, began recognizing and demanding their right to equality. They also realized the advantage of collective over individual action: 'If we form a Women's Association and everyone tells their bitterness in public, no one will dare to oppress you or any woman again,' stated one rural woman (Belden, 1949, p. 24).

The new Women's Associations also utilized group action to punish wife abuse, sometimes temporarily imprisoning and/or physically beating abusive men. However, the Women's Associations did not need to imprison or beat every abuser. Sometimes the mere threat of a confrontation with the Women's Association was usually enough. In the village of Fanshen, for instance, the Women's Association beat several violent husbands. After that, the women only needed to have a 'serious talk' with the abuser to change his behavior (Hinton, 1966, p. 159).

Contemporary organizing against gender violence

Recent legislation, such as the U.S. Violence Against Women Act (1994), recognizes the problem of gender violence and seeks to increase police responsiveness. However, legislation does little to protect women who are politically, economically, or socially marginalized. Instead, the focus on criminalization and incarceration often places them at further risk of both interpersonal and state violence as well as of arrest, incarceration, and, for immigrant women, deportation (Critical Resistance and INCITE! 2001).

Knowing this, women have acted both individually and collectively to defend themselves. Sex workers, for instance, have organized in different ways to protect themselves from violence.

Some methods are fairly straightforward. In March 2006, police responded to the murders of three sex workers in Daytona Beach, Florida, by cracking down on prostitution. In one weekend, 10 people were arrested in a prostitution sting. Recognizing that the police response did more to target than to protect them, street prostitutes began arming themselves with knives and other weapons to both to protect themselves and each other and to find the killer. 'We will get him first,' declared Tonya Richardson, a Ridgewood Avenue prostitute, to Local 6 News. 'When we find him, he is going to be sorry. It is as simple as that' ('Daytona Prostitutes,' 2006).

In Montreal, sex workers have taken a different approach to ensure their safety. In 1995, sex workers, public health researchers, and sympathizers formed Stella, a sex workers' alliance. Instead of knives and other weapons, the group arms sex workers with information and support to help them keep safe. Stella compiles, updates, and circulates a Bad Tricks and Assaulters list, enabling sex workers to share information and avoid dangerous situations. It also produces and provides free reference guides that cover working conditions, current solicitation laws, and health information. Recognizing that the criminalization of activities related to the sex industry renders sex workers vulnerable to both outside violence and police abuse, the group also advocates for the decriminalization of these acts (Stella, n.d.).

Sex workers are also taking direct action to stop sex trafficking. In 1997, former sex workers began guarding checkpoints along the Nepal–India border to rescue adolescent Nepalese girls from being smuggled into India. The idea emerged with the women living at Maiti Nepal, a home in Kathmandu for women returning from Indian brothels. Many of the women, who had been kidnapped as adolescents and sold into the sex industry, were ashamed and angry about their experiences and wanted to transform their anger into action. They set up four guard posts along the border and began monitoring for human trafficking. During the first three years, the women caught 70 traffickers, saving 240 girls from India's brothels.

'All the girls want to go to the border,' stated Anuradha Koirala, who runs Maiti Nepal. 'They are angry but don't know how to express themselves.' Being able to rescue others from similar fates has helped many of the women reclaim their sense of self-worth: at the age of 14, Sushma Katuwal was sold to an Indian brothel where she was infected with HIV. After being held for 13 months, she returned to Kathmandu. 'I came back from hell,' she recalled. 'I am trying to stop these girls from being sold like I was.' In 2000 alone, the 19-year-old rescued 15 girls and caught four human traffickers. 'As long as I survive, this is what I am going to do,' she declared (Filkins, 2000, p. 1).

Women marginalized by other factors, such as racism and poverty, have also organized to protect themselves against both interpersonal and state violence.

In 2000, the police murders of two young women of color sparked a dialogue about violence against women among members of Sista II Sista, a collective of women of color in Brooklyn, New York. The group's preexisting work had empowered young women of color to identify and work toward solving their own problems. Their response was to form Sistas Liberated Ground, a zone in their neighborhood where crimes against women would not be tolerated. 'We wanted the community to stand up against violence as a long-term solution because our dependence on a police system that was inherently sexist, homophobic, racist, and classist did not decrease the ongoing violence against women we were seeing in our neighborhoods. In fact, at times, the police themselves were its main perpetrators,' members of the group stated in 2007 (Burrowes, Cousins, Rojas, & Ude, 2007, p. 229). Sista II Sista instituted an 'action line,' which women could call, inform the group about violence in their lives, and explore the options that they – and the group – could take to change the situation. In addition, Sista II Sista established Sister Circles which, similar to the 'speak bitterness' meetings of the Communist Women's Associations in China, allowed women to talk about violence and other problems in their daily lives and encouraged the community – rather than the individual woman – to find solutions.

In one instance, a woman at the Sister Circle talked about the man who had been stalking her for over a year. Although no physical violence had occurred, he was becoming increasingly aggressive toward her. Members of the Sister Circle confronted the man at the barbershop where he worked. When they learned about his actions, his male co-workers told the stalker that, if he continued to harass the woman, he would be fired. He stopped stalking her (Ude, 2006).

Creating communities to deter violence

Not all strategies to prevent gender violence are easily classified as 'policing from below.' Some grassroots groups and coalitions recognize that building communities is the first line of defense against violence and are organizing to create social structures and support networks that can collectively address harmful situations.

In Durham, North Carolina, in the aftermath of the 2006 rape of a Black woman by members of a Duke University lacrosse team, women of color and survivors of sexual violence formed UBUNTU. UBUNTU, named after the Bantu meaning 'I am because we are,' is a coalition working to 'facilitate a systematic transformation of our communities until the day that sexual violence does not occur' (UBUNTU). Alexis Pauline Gumbs recounted an instance in which an UBUNTU member encountered a woman who had been beaten by her former partner:

> This UBUNTU member called the rest of us to see who was home and available in the direct neighborhood, took the young woman into her home and contacted the spiritual leader of the woman who had experienced the violence along with other women that the young woman trusted from her spiritual community, who also came to the home, and made sure that she was able to receive medical care. She also arranged for members of our UBUNTU family to have a tea session with the young woman to talk about healing and options, to share our experiences, to embrace the young woman and to let her know that she wasn't alone in her healing process. (Piepzna-Samarasinha, 2008, pp. 80–81)

Gumbs noted:

> These responses were invented on the spot … without a pre-existing model or a logistical agreement. But they were also made possible by a larger agreement that we as a collective of people living all over the city are committed to responding to gendered violence. This comes out of the political education and collective healing work that we have done, and the building of relationships that strongly send the message … you can call me if you need something, or if you don't. You can call me to be there for you … or someone that you need help being there for. I think it is very important that we have been able to see each other as resources so that when we are faced with violent situations we don't think our only option is to call the state.
>
> In that way, everything that we do to create community, from childcare to community gardening (our new project!), to community dinners, to film screenings, to political discussions helps to clarify how, why, and how deeply we are ready to be there for each other in times of violence and celebration. (Piepzna-Samarasinha, 2008, p. 81)

From this community-building, UBUNTU members began organizing around the idea of a Harm-Free Zone – an area in which violence would be addressed by the community rather than by the police.

'We shall see [what this looks like in practice] because we're still at the beginning of it,' stated Gumbs in 2009, a year after the idea of a Harm-Free Zone emerged. 'A lot of times we talk about community as if it already exists, but I don't actually think that we have autonomous, completely sustained community. We live with all sorts of dependence on the state, [on] outside institutions. We have a lot of work to do to have the type of communications and support that would fulfill the needs of our community.'

Like the Dorchester Green Light Program, organizers of the Harm-Free Zone brought these ideas to the communities of which they were already a part. 'Those of us who came together were already working in those settings, so it wasn't just [us] going and taking over the local elementary school. Somebody's mom was inspired by what somebody [on the committee] said and invited them to come and speak at [the school's] Women's History Month,' recalled Gumbs. 'For each of us, we're thinking about how we bring that analysis and that ideal into our preexisting communities.'

Conclusion

Many early anti-violence efforts addressed immediate instances of gender violence, often focusing on the physical aspects of self-defense or a direct response to violence. Women's organizations taught self-defense classes, confronted abusers and assailants, and formed protective groups to escort each other safely through the streets. In contrast, contemporary organizing often utilizes a multilayered approach, creatively addressing not only immediate instances of violence but also creating dialogue to challenge and change some of the root causes of gender violence. For instance, the efforts of Stella and UBUNTU are not traditionally seen as self-defense tactics, but they do work to keep women safe from violence. Despite these differences, each project emphasizes the importance of community – as opposed to individual – actions and responses. None of these projects – from the Women's Associations of the 1920s and 1940s to the Dorchester Green Light program in Massachusetts to the contemporary organizing among sex workers – would have succeeded without a collective sense of responsibility toward each other.

Alexis Pauline Gumbs has described UBUNTU's fledgling Harm-Free Zone as 'building safety from the ground up': 'When we say "from the ground up," [we're talking about] really participating in the full life of a community and not just creating a special utopia of ten friends who have a vision that's so abolitionist and radical,' she elaborated.

Annie Ellman also talked about the importance of community and community-building: 'What people gain here [at BWMA] besides self-defense skills is some understanding about collective action, about struggling with your community … If we believe that people have the right to live free of violence, we have to work together to try to transform our communities as ones who will stand up and fight against different kinds of injustice.'

While not every project and group explicitly identifies as an abolitionist group, their practices work toward a radical re-envisioning of creating safety without relying on police. In addition, some groups do work with other antiviolence and abolitionist organizations.

BWMA has, at times, joined in coalition work against police brutality and in support of Mumia Abu-Jamal as well as women incarcerated for self-defense. By the time it changed its name in 1989, CAE had broadened its focus to teach self-defense to other populations disproportionately impacted by violence such as gay men, transgender people, people living with HIV and AIDS, and queer homeless youth (of all genders). 'What we often do is we go out and do educational work for organizations that are more on the front lines doing organizing work,' stated Ellman. After 9/11 increased racist violence against Arab American, South Asian, and Muslim communities, CAE provided free self-defense and violence prevention workshops to women at grassroots organizations that served these communities ('Spotlight on Community Action,' 2004, p. 19).

Alexis Pauline Gumbs noted that UBUNTU's Harm-Free Zone organizing was inspired and influenced by Critical Resistance organizing: one member had previously helped organize a Harm-Free Zone with the New York City Critical Resistance chapter and several people were part of both the Durham chapter of Critical Resistance and the Harm-Free Zone organizing committee.

Although each of the initiatives described works specifically in certain communities, there is the potential for these models to be shared and adapted to other locations and situations.

Gumbs pointed to the Gulabi Gang, a group of women in India who physically punish abusive husbands, and to Sistahs Liberated Ground as inspirations for the Harm-Free Zone organizing in Durham: 'We understand that work in that context while also understanding that our conditions are really specific.'

Other groups have also drawn on past and present models of collective action and community accountability processes. The 1970s German women's group Fan-Shen derived its name from the model Chinese village where Women's Associations stopped wife abuse. More recently, activists in Santa Cruz were influenced by a documentary about a 1970s feminist group that collectively confronted sexual assaulters, forming Snap Back! in 2002. Snap Back! members used a similar tactic to confront a man who had sexually assaulted their friend. 'We went to his house at night with her and we made him come outside,' recalled Snap Back! member Megan Reed. 'She talked to him about what had happened while the rest of us stood there showing solidarity with her. She decided to go inside to have a longer conversation with him (about an hour). Then we left.'

Although nothing more happened, Reed believed that their action had further-reaching effects: 'I think it scared the crap out of him and he'll think twice before doing anything like that again,' she stated. The action also 'gave her [the survivor] a sense of closure. If you don't want to go through the legal system, there are few alternatives as to what you can do to get closure and confront that person and feel that a politically justifiable result has been attained.' Knowledge about a past group's approaches toward sexual assault enabled Snap Back! members to help their friend confront her assailant in a way that did not involve the police or prisons.

'Where Abolition Meets Actions' utilizes Mimi Kim's storytelling approach to envision different possibilities of a world without policing and prisons. These models are important for imagining and then realizing abolitionist principles. By examining the variety of approaches in their vastly different contexts, we can begin to connect the abstract ideal with concrete actions that make another world possible. We should be drawing lessons from these projects and approaches to create models that work for our own locations and communities.

Acknowledgments

As an independent researcher, I am blessed to have a network of friends, writers, and activists who provide crucial support. For this article, I owe much thanks and appreciation to China Martens for feedback on early drafts, Jessica Ross for introducing me to several of the women interviewed as well as extensive feedback, and Jenna Freedman for material support. This article could not have been written without them.

References

Belden, J. (1949). *China shakes the world.* New York: Harper.

Burrowes, N., Cousins, M., Rojas, P.X., & Ude, I. (2007). On our own terms: 10 years of radical community building with Sista II Sista. In INCITE! Women of Color Against Violence (Ed.), *The revolution will not be funded: Beyond the non-profit industrial complex* (pp. 227–234). Cambridge, MA: South End Press.

Bustamante, C. (1986, May). Planning to end violence against women. *off our backs, 26*(5), 14.
Critical Resistance and INCITE! (2001). *Critical Resistance – INCITE! Statement on gender violence and the prison industrial complex.* Retrieved from http://www.incite-national.org/index.php?s=92
Croll, E. (1978). *Feminism and socialism in China.* London: Routledge & Kegan Paul.
Daytona Prostitutes Hunting Serial Killer. (2006, March 13). *Orlando News.* Retrieved from http://www.clickorlando.com/news/7977302/detail.html
Dejanikus, T., & Kelly, J. (1979). Roxbury organizing. *off our backs, 9*(9), 7.
Dunbar-Ortiz, R. (2001). *Outlaw woman: A memoir of the war years, 1960–1975.* San Francisco, CA: City Lights.
Filkins, D. (2000, June 26). On guard against a flesh trade. *Los Angeles Times*, p. 1.
Giggans, P.O. (1994). In search of solid ground: Women's response to violence. *Iris, 31*, 41.
Hinton, W. (1966). *Fanshen: A documentary of revolution in a Chinese village.* New York: Monthly Review Press.
Honig, E. (1997). Burning incense, pledging sisterhood: Communities of women workers in Shanghai cotton mills, 1919–1949. In V. Taylor, L. Richardson, & N. Whittiers (Eds.), *Feminist frontiers* (pp. 485–493). New York: McGraw-Hill.
Huang, V. (2008). Transforming communities: Community-based responses to partner abuse. In C.-I. Chen, J. Dulani, & L. Piepzna-Samarasinha (Eds.), *The revolution starts at home: Confronting partner abuse in activist communities* [zine] (pp. 58–63). Oakland, CA: The editors.
Lafferty, J., & Clark, E. (1970). Self-defense and the preservation of females. *No More Fun and Games: A Journal of Female Liberation*, No. 3, 96–97.
Lehmann, N. (1975). Consider a future for self-defense. *Black Belt Woman, 2*, 19.
Piepzna-Samarasinha, L. (2008). An interview with Alexis Paulina Gumbs of UBUNTU. In C.-I. Chen, J. Dulani, & L. Piepzna-Samarasinha (Eds.), *The revolution starts at home: Confronting partner abuse in activist communities* (pp. 80–82). Oakland, CA: The editors.
Smith, A. (2005). *Conquest: Sexual violence and American Indian genocide.* Cambridge, MA: South End Press.
Spotlight on Community Action. (2004). *From strength of strength: Celebrating 30 years of vision and leadership.* Brooklyn, NY: Center for Anti-Violence Education.
Stella. (n.d.). *Who are we?* Retrieved from http://www.chezstella.org/stella/?q=en/tools
Strong, A.L. (1928). *China's millions.* New York: Coward-McCann.
UBUNTU. (n.d.). *About UBUNTU.* Retrieved from http://iambecauseweare.wordpress.com/
Ude, I. (2006, April 8). *Changing actions.* Panel discussion at the Scholar and Feminist Conference XXXI: Engendering Justice – Prisons, Activism and Change, Barnard College, NY.
Women's Patrol Ousts Beaters. (1977). *The Lesbian Tide*, p. 18.

Corking as community policing

Jeff Ferrell

Department of Sociology, Texas Christian University, Fort Worth, Texas, USA

Over the past couple of decades there has emerged a new generation of movements for social justice that in particular embrace 'direct action' and 'do-it-yourself' activism – that is, the replacing of traditional forms of social movement 'protest' or political agitation with the direct, immediate, and autonomous enactment of the movement's alternative models for living. Among the more successful of these is Critical Mass, a global movement that 'dis-organizes' collective bicycle rides as inclusive and environmentally appropriate alternatives to automotive transit. Within Critical Mass, the dismissal of institutionalized policing power and the embracing of do-it-yourself activism have spawned the practice of 'corking,' whereby a Critical Mass bicyclist breaks away from the collective ride and stops to block a crossing street as the mass of riders rolls through a traffic intersection. The distinctly 'dis-organized' and culturally engaged dynamics of corking have in turn served to construct corking as an informal version of community policing – of policing both the transitory community of Critical Mass riders and the neighborhood communities through which the ride passes.

Over the past couple of decades a new generation of movements for social justice has emerged. While oriented around any number of environmental, economic, and political issues, these movements share certain dynamics that distinguish them from many earlier social movements in the USA and elsewhere. At a fundamental level, such movements embrace 'direct action' and the 'propaganda of the deed' – that is, the notion of replacing traditional forms of social movement 'protest' or agitation toward long-term goals with the direct, immediate enactment of the movement's alternative models for living. From this view, such movements work not to promote their alternative values as ideology but rather to live them as everyday practice – and thus to demonstrate that such alternatives are indeed viable. Animating this approach is a commitment to 'DIY' (do it yourself) social change. Typically, this commitment means that these movements choose to create their own media rather than playing to mainstream media coverage; to work for direct, local change rather than appealing to political authorities for endorsement; and to disavow the need for the permission or assistance of legal authorities in the conducting of movement activities. Finally, these new social movements distinguish themselves from many earlier movements by emphasizing fluid 'dis-organization' over traditional forms of social movement organization. Such dis-organization, these movements emphasize, promotes more inclusive, democratic, and spontaneous forms of activism than are available within more tightly organized social movements, and so inaugurates the very sorts of alternative social arrangements that the movements seek (Ferrell, 2001; McKay, 1998).

Among the more successful of these movements is Critical Mass, which originated in the Bay Area of the USA in the early 1990s and has now spread to hundreds of cities throughout North and South American, Europe, Australia, Asia, and Africa. Critical Mass activists highlight the social atomization and environmental harm spawned by pervasive automotive use in urban areas, and promote bicycling as a more directly inclusive and environmentally appropriate form of urban mobility (Carlsson, 2002). In accordance with the dynamics of such movements, though, Critical Mass activists promote this perspective not through street protests or conventional political activism, but by dis-organizing large, collective bicycle rides in urban areas. These Critical Mass rides, often involving hundreds or thousands of participants, are indeed distinctive in their (lack of) orchestration and execution. Critical Mass has no official leadership through which the collective rides are organized; instead, they come together though 'xerocracy,' a dispersed do-it-yourself media of fliers, emails, phone calls, and websites. Any particular ride itself may or may not be guided by a shared, xeroxed ride map, which riders in turn may or may not follow as the ride unfolds. Further, Critical Mass activists note that these 'organized coincidences' are not meant as pro-bicycle or anti-car protests, but rather as 'celebrations' during which participants can experience, and observers can witness, the possibilities of bicycling as a collective alternative to the car. 'Each ride is different from city to city,' says Klett (2002, p. 90). 'The ride constantly synthesizes the amalgam of desires and allows for collective and individual responses to motorists, pedestrians, bus riders, authorities, and the various neighborhoods through which it passes' (p. 90).

In the context of this emergent, do-it-yourself approach to alternative urban mobility, Critical Mass activists decline to seek prior official permission or parade permits for their rides, or to negotiate with city officials over ride routes or numbers of participants. By the logic of Critical Mass, this disavowal is grounded in the sense that such bureaucratic restrictions would inevitably undermine the spontaneously democratic nature of the rides – but it also grows out of the practical fact that there are no Critical Mass leaders with whom officials can negotiate, and no firm ride routes or participant numbers to be proffered. During the rides themselves, Critical Mass participants neither seek nor claim to need the assistance of local police officers as the riders negotiate issues of ride safety or crowd control. Notably, this Critical Mass approach to police authority is not so much confrontational as dismissive. One Critical Mass activist writes that 'Critical Mass resonates with so many because it exemplifies [the] act of taking matters into one's own hands. It does not protest for change, it simply changes … There is an instinct to protect the right to freely assemble … CM [Critical Mass] takes that right at face value and exercises it. Critical Mass challenges Authority by ignoring it' (Stender, 2002, p. 89). A group of Critical Mass activists are more explicit. 'The best approach to the police presence at Critical Mass,' they argue, 'is not to engage in some pathetic, losing confrontation, or embrace them as our saviors and protectors. Rather, we should ignore them and get on with the business of trying to build a Mass' (D'Andrade et al., 2002, p. 248).

Predictably, perhaps, Critical Mass's non-confrontational dismissal of legal authority has led legal authorities to confront Critical Mass, with Critical Mass rides at times accompanied by citations, arrests, and odd mixes of uninvited police protection and police harassment. In one particularly dramatic case, then-San Francisco

Mayor Willie Brown frustratingly failed in his attempt to identify a Critical Mass leadership with whom he could negotiate route plans and police escorts. As *Time* magazine reported in an article titled 'The Scariest Biker Gang of All,' 'the normally unflappable Mayor Willie Brown, a world-class deal broker, seemed ready to snap. Critical Mass … had got his goat by having no one for him to cut a deal with' (Lopez, 1997, p. 4). And indeed the following San Francisco Critical Mass ride did reveal a certain snapping of legal authority, with local police making hundreds of arrests, confiscating riders' bicycles en masse, and attempting (unsuccessfully) to stop the ride in its entirety.

Yet, Critical Mass's dismissal of institutionalized policing and embracing of do-it-yourself social change has led to something else as well: *corking*. In the terminology of Critical Mass, corking refers to the act of a Critical Mass bicyclist breaking away from the mass and stopping to block a crossing side street as the mass of riders rolls through a traffic intersection. At a minimum, this 'corking' is meant to serve two purposes. First, corking is designed to protect the mass of riders from any motorist who might otherwise get anxious or angry and attempt to drive through the assembled bicyclists. Second, since a mass of hundreds or thousands of bicyclists will generally require more than one green light to make it through an intersection, corking is designed to hold up cross-traffic as the mass continues through a green-light-turned-red, and so to keep the riders together in a 'critical mass.' Once again, the intent is not to confront traffic regulations (though Critical Mass proponents do see them as largely encoding automotive privilege) but to disregard their innate authority. 'Critical Mass should bend or ignore existing traffic laws where the group's safety and effectiveness will be served,' argue Critical Mass activists, 'and follow the law where it serves our interests and needs' (D'Andrade et al., 2002, p. 244).[1]

Beyond this, the distinct social dynamics of corking construct it as an alternative, informal version of community policing – of policing both the transitory community of Critical Mass riders and the neighborhood communities through which the ride passes. As Critical Mass activists take pains to point out – and as I have confirmed in researching and riding with Critical Mass – there exists no pre-set map of intersections to be corked, nor any pre-designated roster of corkers. It remains for the riders themselves to decide when corking is needed, and for each rider to decide when she or he will cork; in this way, corking embodies the disorganized, inclusive democracy of the ride itself, and replicates this orientation through fluid social reinforcement. 'No one has the job of corking,' Critical Mass activist Caycee Cullen explains. 'It's just like as you're going through, people will notice, wow, and just speed up and jump out [to cork], and everybody appreciates that, and then the next time you'll do it. You know, it's an unwritten dynamic' (in Ferrell, 2001, p. 107). For Critical Mass riders, corking operates doubly as a form of do-it-yourself direct action, as participants not only take on the responsibility of policing their own safety, but do so through shared, spontaneous decision-making. Given that Critical Mass's intention is not to 'protest' for social change but rather to enact alternative forms of dis-organized, inclusive urban community, corking in this way emerges as an essential factor in confirming the viability of such liquid, alternative arrangements.

Critical Mass activists are of course aware that corking affects not only the ride participants but the motorists who are delayed by the corking of intersections – and here as well, the goal is to avoid confrontation and invite inclusion. Corkers are understood to be 'the diplomats of the ride' (D'Andrade et al., 2002, p. 243) – that is, those who will most directly engage with non-riders, and so have the opportunity to shape their perceptions of Critical Mass. Consequently, in both the literature of Critical Mass and in informal conversations among riders, corkers are encouraged to smile, make eye contact with motorists, and if possible engage motorists in conversation while they wait. In addition, in anticipation that they or someone else in the ride may well end up corking, riders often carry signs that they can use in corking or pass to other corkers. Reading 'Thank You For Waiting' and 'Honk If You Love Bikes,' these signs are likewise displayed to motorists in an attempt to encourage their cooperation and symbolic support. Though not always successful, the usual effect of such tactics is to diffuse potential conflict between impeded motorists and Critical Mass participants, and to create a culture of calmness in and around the ride. This effect in turn re-enforces another of Critical Mass's ongoing self-policing strategies: the attempt to minimize the influence of the 'testosterone brigade,' those generally young, male Critical Mass riders who might seek confrontation with automobile drivers or police.

Corking in this way serves to police more than the potential for automotive intrusion into a Critical Mass ride; it serves to police the meaning of the ride for participants and spectators alike, and the perceptions that participants and spectators will take from it. Corking is as much community relations as it is traffic control, a do-it-yourself attempt at forging partnerships between Critical Mass and those who occupy the immediate situations that the ride traverses. Relying on moral persuasion more than physical force, engaging a strategy as liquid as the ride itself, Critical Mass participants deploy their own form of alternative community policing. The U.S. Department of Justice (2010) defines community policing as 'a philosophy that promotes organizational strategies which support the systematic use of partnerships and problem-solving techniques, to proactively address the immediate conditions that give rise to public safety issues such as crime, social disorder, and fear of crime.' While no doubt denying the authority of the Department of Justice to define the nature of justice or community or policing, Critical Mass activists might otherwise agree – so long as they could cut those 'organizational strategies' with a big does of on-the-fly dis-organization.

Note

1. Similarly, Critical Mass and Reclaim the Streets activists on occasion alter STOP signs such that they come to read, 'STOP DRIVING' (Ferrell, 2001, pp. 97–99).

References

Carlsson, C. (Ed.). (2002). *Critical mass.* Edinburgh: AK Press.

D'Andrade, H., Verdekal, B., Carlsson, C., Swanson, J.R., Roberts, K., & French, N. (2002). How to make a Critical Mass. In C. Carlsson (Ed.), *Critical mass* (pp. 239–248). Edinburgh: AK Press.

Ferrell, J. (2001). *Tearing down the streets.* New York: Palgrave.

Klett, M. (2002). A uniquely democratic experiment. In C. Carlsson (Ed.), *Critical mass* (pp. 90–93). Edinburgh: AK Press.

Lopez, S. (1997, August 11). The scariest biker gang of all. *Time, 150*, 4.

McKay, G. (1998). *DIY culture.* London: Verso.

Stender, B. (2002). From the ground up. In C. Carlsson (Ed.), *Critical mass* (pp. 87–89). Edinburgh: AK Press.

U.S. Department of Justice. (2010). *Community policing defined.* Retrieved April 18, 2010, from http://www.cops.usdoj.gov/default.asp?item=36

Index

For Product Safety Concerns and Information please contact our EU representative GPSR@taylorandfrancis.com Taylor & Francis Verlag GmbH, Kaufingerstraße 24, 80331 München, Germany

Printed and bound by CPI Group (UK) Ltd, Croydon, CR0 4YY
14/09/2026
02216246-0001